Psychology Exposed

Psychology Exposed or The Emperor's New Clothes

Paul Kline

R

Routledge
London and New York

First published in 1988 by
Routledge
11 New Fetter Lane, London EC4P 4EE

Published in the USA by
Routledge
in association with Routledge, Chapman and Hall, Inc.
29 West 35th Street, New York NY10001

Set in 10/12 pt Times by Input Typesetting Ltd, London
and printed in Great Britain by Biddles Ltd, Guildford & Kings Lynn.

British Library Cataloguing in Publication Data

Kline, Paul, 1937-
　　Psychology exposed, or, The emperor's new clothes.
　　1. Psychology
　　I. Title
　　150

Library of Congress Cataloging in Publication Data

Kline, Paul.
Psychology exposed, or, The emperor's new clothes / Paul Kline.
p.　cm.
Bibliography: p.
Includes index.
1. Psychology, Experimental. 2. Psychology–Research–Methodology.
I. Title. II. Title: Emperor's new clothes. BF181.K52 1988
152′.01–dc19

ISBN 0–415–00643–0
ISBN 0–415–00644–9 Pbk

Contents

Preface

However, it is difficult to avoid being trivial in verbal
discussions of the complexity of the interactions. Accordingly
we are developing a formal notation . . . (Morton, 1987)

I have written this book, *Psychology Exposed, or The Emperor's
New Clothes* after twenty-five years as an academic psychologist,
during which time I committed most of the sins which I describe
in its pages. Its writing, therefore, resembles a confession which
is to its author both horrifying and pleasant, easing the burden of
intellectual guilt. As with all confessions, it enrages those who
recognize in themselves the same guilt but are not yet ready for
repentance. The aim of this book, therefore, is simply to reduce
Augustine's time gap to zero – please God let me be chaste, but
not yet – for in my view unless academic psychology does rapidly
change, the subject will disappear for ever, relegated to the dimension of intellectual rubbish which includes such glories as
iridology, phrenology, necromancy, and coprology.

Chapter one

The problem

The problem which constitutes the core of this book is the disjunction of experimental psychology as a science and the nature of man. It will be argued that as it has now been developed experimental psychology is unable to come to grips with what is essentially human and that the further it appears to progress, the further away in fact it flees from what should be the natural objective of psychology. As a result of this, modern psychology is not only valueless, but actually corrosive, destroying any possibility of insight into human behaviour.

To demonstrate this point it will be necessary to examine the nature of experimental psychology, in all its manifold branches, and, of course, the nature of man. Clearly all psychological methods have to be judged against the criterion of man's nature and this is the main topic of this introductory chapter.

The nature of man

One of the difficulties which psychology has always to face is that there are so many views of man which, if accepted, lead to methods and approaches in psychology which have little in common. There is the religious view in which man is unique, lit by a divine spark and, perhaps, tainted by Original Sin. Such a viewpoint given the dominance of Roman Catholicism and the Muslim religion is still probably that of the majority of people. In direct contrast to this, as was the case at the time of Darwin, is what might be called the evolutionary position in which man is regarded as another animal, more highly evolved in respect of cortical function than any other but still an animal; possibly,

1

judging from his history, the worst animal in the world. This is the viewpoint of ethologists, who study behaviour as it naturally occurs, and of animal psychologists who investigate their subjects in the laboratory. However, as I shall demonstrate, interesting and fascinating as this work may be in its own right, it is not possible to generalize from animals to man, even if their evolutionary unity is accepted. Obviously, it goes without saying, those who believe in the Divinity of Man will not bother with animal psychology as a guide to man's behaviour.

However, even if it is agreed that the only route to understanding man is to study man, there are still so many viewpoints underpinned by so many different assumptions that no approach is beyond dispute. In the Skinnerian view, for example, man is essentially a plastic organism shaped by his environment. He learns what he is reinforced to learn. Obviously here the central study of psychology must be *learning*. This kind of psychology is discussed in Chapter 7, as is the animal work with its implication that man and animals are one.

A view that is clearly, but not entirely, opposed to this is the genetical view of human behaviour which, as the name suggests, argues that much of human behaviour is largely genetically determined although environmental interaction is always allowed for. This is an ancient doctrine and in its modern form is embodied in psychometrics which has isolated a number of important factors in human behaviour, factors which show a high hereditary determination. Intelligence and extraversion are two such factors. This work is fully discussed in Chapter 4.

One view of man stands out in the twentieth century, the Freudian psychoanalytic view which indeed changed the *Zeitgeist*. Man once seen through the psychoanalytic lens never looks the same again. Experimental psychology has dismissed this viewpoint as hopelessly unscientific and therefore to be ignored, despite its enormous influence on the way we think. This refusal to take this model of man into account is one of the root causes of the evils of experimental psychology, as I demonstrate throughout this book.

Perhaps because psychoanalysis has failed to live up to the exaggerated claims of its adherents, for it is no cure for the ills that beset our society, and because of the constant sniping of scientists, in scientific circles psychoanalysis is not what once it was. Today Freud would not be elected into the Royal Society. In its place among the scientific *cognoscenti* a new approach or model of man has become the rage. This is man the computer. Based upon this approach departments of artificial intelligence and cognitive science have sprung into being attracting huge funds, a sign stimulus for scientists. In this model man is seen as an information processing machine, as is the computer; a Turing machine, as specified in the 1930s. The flaws and errors in this approach which has recently informed cognitive psychology as well, I deal with in Chapter 6, and in Chapter 2 cognitive models are dealt with which are implicitly rather than explicitly computational.

On entirely different dimensions, cutting right across these approaches which I have discussed, is the old dispute between introspective and behaviourist schools of psychology. Here the argument was whether science had to be concerned with observable public events or could deal with the inferences and constructs necessary if mental processes were to be discussed. At one point in British psychology, at least, it seemed as if behaviourism had the upper hand and this was the basic assumption of learning theoretic accounts of behaviour. However, computational and cognitive psychology are clearly not behaviourist in this traditional sense. The behavourist approach was closely bound up with the conception of science and scientific method current at that time – a univariate rather than a multivariate concept of science.

The emphasis of behaviourism on science, and thus the psychological laboratory, led to the development of social psychology which very sensibly argued that as behaviour always occurs within some context, and it is obvious that the context influences what we do and say, behaviour and its context must be studied together. This is what social psychology attempts to do in a scientific and experimental way. It is this work I examine in Chapter 5: man the social animal.

Since I am arguing that the diverse views of man strongly affect the psychological research that is done and held to be important there is a view of man which must be mentioned, certainly as influential as that of Freud in the twentieth century and one which ostensibly has profoundly affected the lives of millions of people throughout the world. This is, of course, the Marxist view of man, economic man, motivated by financial gain, although in the

Marxist argument this is the result of the conditioning of capitalist society. It is fair to say that in American and European society these views have not influenced experimental psychology, although I suppose that the study of reinforcers might be related to it.

Finally one other approach to psychology should be briefly discussed. This is the reductionist or physiological approach which seeks to understand human psychology in terms of its underlying physiology. For example, in the study of the perception of straight lines and curves individual edge detectors have been found in the visual cortex (work that has won the Nobel Prize) and how these are used in visual perception has been impressively hypothesized. However, I should like to make two points here. The first is that this work is really physiology. It describes the physiology of vision, how we see. However, in perception there must be corresponding physiological changes, yet these changes *are not* identical with perception. The experience of these perceptions, not these physiological changes, constitutes the psychology and to this by definition, physiology can have nothing to say. This is the reason I regard these often brilliant studies of perceptual phenomena as physiology rather than psychology and for this reason they fall beyond the purview of my book.

I think that I have written sufficient to show that there are indeed a diversity of views of man and that each produces in its train a particular view of what is worthy of study and in some instances of how it should be studied. I have dealt with this problem in two ways which together, I hope, largely overcome it. In the first instance I ignore this problem, examining man from a viewpoint that is relevant to psychology. I look at those activities which universally seem important. By so doing this almost defines the nature of man. However, since experimental psychology stems from views of man, as I have discussed, which are different from this and depend on various assumptions, I also examine these different branches of psychology in later chapters of the book. I do not want to fall foul of the perfectly reasonable argument that my definition of man is such that all experimental psychology must fail to deal with the subject matter.

Nevertheless, despite this complication, I think that defining man by listing what is important to him gives us a clear idea of what experimental psychology should be concerned with. I shall now simply list, therefore, a number of activities which almost all individuals do and which, by common agreement in most cultures of the world, seem important to them.

Human activities

Although I suppose that a truly exhaustive list of human activities would have to include all verbs in all languages, a sample which I and my friends enjoy is illuminating enough: eating, drinking and having sex – the basic biological necessities together with breathing, excreting and defecating which are enjoyed especially by certain groups, as is alleged in psychoanalysis. Then there are the more social pleasures of laughing and talking, exercising, running, swimming, competing, sleeping and dreaming, weeping. Writing, making music, playing chess or bridge, feeling drunk, skiing, driving fast, being pampered, being mothered, mothering, giving orders and being ordered, listening to music, watching cricket, bird-watching – but enough is enough. This tiny vignette of what a person may do indicates, at least, the richness of human behaviour, its diversity and scope and already I can hear readers note the cultural, university bias – what about football and cooking, playing bingo and betting, eating fish and chips from a newspaper, reading bad books, pornography, adultery.

This virtually random list, activities which spring to mind as constituting the pleasure of life and sometimes its woes, is extensive and variegated; nevertheless there are other human pursuits which are virtually universal. Life is, to quote Sweeney, but birth, copulation, death. In virtually all societies children have to be reared; individuals have to learn the mores of their society (being educated) and have to work to earn their living. Language is universal with all that implies for self-expression. Joy and woe is the human condition, as a response to which arises religion or its modern substitute of a political philosophy.

Such a list as this reveals perhaps an academic psychological or behaviouristic bias in that the description of man has been conceptualized or realized as activities. This, however, would give a false impression. It was intended to adumbrate the scope and diversity of human behaviour, a breadth which any experimental psychology should capture. However, as we all know, there is more to life than acting. Sometimes I just sits and thinks, and

5

then again sometimes I just sits. This always raises a laugh of some kind, and one could well ask why. What is amusing about just sitting? I think that it is its difficulty. Many of us would love to be able to just sit, to banish the painful contents of our heads but, alas, we cannot. Hence the humour of the phrase, the simpleton doing what we, so much wiser, would like but cannot do. This is the humour, therefore, of juxtaposition and the humour of the expression of a longed for desire.

I raise this because it demonstrates that behaviour, overt activity, can never wholly describe a person. Thoughts and feelings are often the most important thing in life. Loving, being in love, to many this is all that matters. The content of popular songs, of poetry and the arts is love, and with love goes hate, and with hate aggression and violence. Feelings, then, must constitute a part of any psychology of man. A list of feelings or emotions is indeed revelatory. Love and hate I have mentioned, rage, anger, anxiety, sadness, and grief, joy, happiness, depression, and the Black Dog that lopes behind our lives. No, it is obvious that a psychology of behaviour alone is inadequate. A psychology of feeling is a necessity.

Another approach to gaining some insight into the diversity of human behaviour and the complexity of the psyche is to examine the content of newspapers. Some of what may be discovered has been, naturally enough, discussed in the paragraphs above, and it would be very odd if that were not the case. Different ways of looking at human beings should show some agreement. Newspapers, given that there is any truth in their reports, must show two things. They indicate what people actually do, and they indicate what editors believe people like to read about (and it is not much, given the content of many papers). If we assume that people do like reading the popular press (and are not the gullible persons of capitalistic advertising as Marxists would have us believe – how odd that advocates of the working man have so low an opinion of him) newspaper content is thus a useful indicant of human behaviour. On these criteria murder, sex, observing the Royal Family at play, wars, disasters, and accidents vicariously experienced, rape and crime are all of immense human significance. So too is astrology, parapsychology, and the occult. In the sense of what people do, the subject matter of the press, killing especially in the name of religion, fanatical religious belief, and violence of every sort familial and for the sake of drugs and drink, adultery, these are what people do and these are the things in which people are interested. This interest, indeed, from a psychoanalytic viewpoint, strongly suggests that, since the majority of what are conveniently called decent people do not indulge these activities, many people would like so to do.

What the more thoughtful and intellectually aspiring sections of the media concern themselves with is also of significance for this broad delineation of human behaviour, in its widest sense embracing thoughts and emotions as well as 'observable behaviour', the chimera of academic psychology. Here we find coverage of such psychological questions as the nature and cause of mental illness and its treatment, the psychological aspects of physical disease, the question of racial differences, whether they exist and if they do their provenance in genes and culture. Indeed the very nature of man is examined. Is he religious? How can he be controlled or persuaded? Is he inevitably flawed? Original sin is still a fundamental issue.

I do not think that there can be much doubt that all the concerns and deeds of humanity that I have listed in this simple delineation of what it is to be human constitute an accurate picture of what people do and what people enjoy and like to understand. Nor is this term 'understand' chosen lightly or by accident, for the very existence of the media and institutions of learning, indeed the very presence of language in man, I take as evidence for a faculty which is of enormous significance, and that is a wish or need to understand the world, which may be learned or may be built in, an evolutionary advantage in the terms of sociobiology, a product of man's huge cortex.

Academic psychology

Such, then, is the subject matter of psychology, if this is to be the study of man. Yet as I indicated in the opening lines of this chapter, there is a terrible disjunction. Scientific psychology, as it is now conceived in universities in the west and almost throughout the world, barely seems to touch upon these issues.

Let me exemplify the point by examining the titles of papers in journals and conferences. I shall not here make the kind of detailed search of all journals and all conferences that a careful academic would demand, in order to prove this point. At this juncture I shall scrutinize two recent conferences. The first was concerned with developmental psychology, the second with personality, both topics surely relevant to life and not the province of esoteric science as perhaps might be justified in the study, say, of the biochemistry of nerve conduction.

Some titles of conference papers

I shall take first the 1985 Annual Conference of the Developmental Section of the British Psychological Society. There were approximately 100 papers in the programme. I will examine a few of the papers, for instance, 'The development of classificatory behaviours of language concepts and visual shapes among high and low socio-economic status children'. Apart from the incomprehensibility of the title, the research itself raises a number of fundamental issues. Why take high and low socio-economic class children? The fact that a child's parents have a good or bad job tells us, *per se*, nothing about the way they rear their children. Even if differences between the groups are observed, it is psychologically meaningless unless what these parents do or do not do is related to the development of classificatory behaviours. Thus the topic is bound to yield no information. Furthermore, so narrow is the development of classificatory behaviours of language concepts and visual shapes, that generalizability is impossible. Again one could ask, what is a visual shape? What shape is not visual? Perhaps even more significant than these severe weaknesses of the research topic, is the limited narrow scope of the subject itself. This topic was not to be found in our delineation of the nature of man.

The next paper in this session on cognitive development was entitled 'Children's understanding of the conservation experiment: content, capacity, and causal attributions'. In this case the limited topic is a clear example of my claimed disjunction. This paper is a study of the 'Conservation Experiment', an experiment first performed by Piaget to demonstrate that at a certain stage of intellectual development, children had no grasp of capacity – that amounts of, say, water remain the same when put in tall thin jars or broad jars. Before the development of conservation children are deceived by appearances. Although interesting and perhaps ingenious, the conservation experiment would not appear to be one of the more significant aspects of human behaviour. Remember that psychologists choose their experiments. They could study anything they like.

After coffee, on the first day, a paper, 'Children's recall strategies in collaborative working arrangements' (presumably working together), was presented. However well executed, it could not be argued that such a subject could add much to knowledge of human behaviour. To the question of why one might want to discover such knowledge, a meaningful answer would be difficult.

After tea, two papers were programmed, one on 'Vegetable equilibrium: Piaget and plant psychology', and a second entitled 'Spontaneous metric measurement in five year olds'. The former was not entirely serious, the author informs me, but it is certainly of little interest to students of human behaviour as it has been delineated earlier in the chapter. It is not, *per se*, particularly funny either, although this must be a matter of personal values. Nor would the second paper appear to impinge on many of the subjects deemed to be of wide significance. It is obvious, and it would be wearisome to continue the case, that these papers are not concerned with topics in psychology that non-psychologists, at least, consider to be important.

Of course not all the titles of the papers were so clearly concerned with narrow and ultimately trivial topics but, even where this was not the case, the research was such as to make generalization extremely difficult, if not absolutely impossible.

I do not want to say more about this conference on developmental psychology. It is sufficient to note that these experiments cannot be regarded as highly germane to what most people believe to be important in human behaviour.

I shall now turn to the International Conference in the study of Personality which was held in Gdansk, Poland in 1985. Regrettably in this conference there was a similar disjunction between the papers and what appears to be important psychology. Again I shall illustrate my point by examining some of the papers presented – this time by psychologists from eastern and western Europe – different intellectual traditions within the subject.

In the conference two days were devoted to studies of the 'self'. A paper was presented – 'The Self as an organized system of valuations'. Even if it could be shown that the self could be construed as an organized system of valuations, it is pertinent to enquire where such a categorization is likely to lead. This seems remarkably like an academic exercise done entirely for its own sake. Similarly 'The Self in drug addicts' would not appear to have much potential. Are drug addicts addicted because of their 'self' or is their 'self' affected by their addiction? In either case what does it truly tell us about the nature of addiction, especially since, in any case, measures of the concept of the self are not noted for either their reliability or validity.

In the section devoted to miscellaneous research, there can be found a paper entitled 'Visual perception similarities between children and anxiety and obsessive neurotics'. Whatever these similarities be, it is difficult to see how there can be much of theoretical or practical utility in the results. What can be made of the fact that they are or are not similar? A further study concerned 'Self-acceptance and acceptance of others as personality variables in France, West Germany, and White South Africa – a cross-cultural study'. Once again one must question how important are the variables of self-acceptance and acceptance of others, given the infinity of possible variables to investigate. Futhermore, a cross-cultural study comprising results in three cultures is certainly interesting although any differences would have to be tied down to actual differences in the cultures. These are by no means easy to measure, and may require several years of anthropological investigation even to discern.

Another paper was presented on 'Planetary temperament – discovery or artefact'. This is of interest to a large number of people. Indeed given the postulates of different religions over the world – Hinduism and Buddhism for example – it is almost certainly true to say that the majority of people believe in the tenets of astrology, that their lives and characteristics are affected by the motion of the planets. Thus this is an instance of scientific research being in accord with popular notions of psychology. However it is noteworthy that astrological research is heavily played down in academic psychology. It is part of few courses for degrees in psychology, and to venture into it is inevitably regarded in the scientific world as evidence of crankiness, senility, and a general failure of cerebration. What research there is is actually extremely limited, restricted to investigating season of birth, essentially, and personality characteristics.

I have omitted mentioning from both conferences all those papers which are highly technical or use jargon which is quite impenetrable other than to specialists in those particular fields. However, it can safely be said that such research highlights, if anything more strongly than the papers whose titles I have cited, this divorce of scientific psychology from what would appear to be its natural subject matter. One paper, albeit simple, on astrological influences on personality, did seem to deal with what has always been of great interest in most cultures, and as I have indicated, astrology together with all branches of parapsychology is virtually never studied in academic departments of psychology.

Conclusions

It is clear from this simple initial survey that academic psychology, as illustrated by these two recent conferences on essentially humane psychology is not concerned with what appear to non-psychologists to be the most important or interesting aspects of being human. This, in my view, is the cause of the failure of psychology to offer anything of intellectual or practical value. As I shall argue, academic psychology is a collection of results, I cannot call it knowledge, that is of no interest, value or use except to other academic psychologists who for reasons of furthering their careers and in some cases on account of their own psycho-pathology take it upon themselves to pursue this research. Additional pressures to produce an apparently endless flow of papers, an infinite flux, come from the nature of the educational institutions in which they operate – counters of pages rather than assessors of intellectual ideas.

However, the fact that there is this apparently unbridgeable chasm between the subject matter of academic psychology and what to a sane and rational person seems to be important is not *proof per se* that the whole pursuit of psychology is worthless – although this is my contention. It could be the case that the special methods of academic psychology in the various branches of the subject are extremely powerful in yielding knowledge. For example, the naïve observer of the natural world would not expect that a study of atomic particles would be valuable in understanding it. Yet theoretical and experimental physics has indubitably advanced knowledge of the world to such an extent that we are able and ready to destroy it. Furthermore, it is an arrogant and dogmatic assertion to claim, because of the disjunction of the subject matters to which I have referred, that academic psychology cannot succeed. Academic psychologists must and do have their own explicit ostensible rationale for their work.

Thus in the succeeding chapters of this book, I will examine the rationale of the scientific methods adopted by psychologists and demonstrate them to be wanting and will show in addition that the methods are not appropriate for the study of psychology, and that as applied in the manifold fields of psychology, they are doomed to failure. Finally, I will argue that firm, sound knowledge of psychology is possible, if the absurd prejudices, antiquated thinking, and obsessional pedantry of psychology are abandoned and replaced by thought.

Chapter two

What the scientific method is and why psychologists use it

The essence of academic life is dispute. Mediaeval scholars debated how many angels could sit upon the head of a pin, a matter that has still not been finally resolved. This great tradition lives on and thus a clear statement of a position is the life blood of the academic world. It will be seized upon with as much avidity as intellectual torpor allows (all things are relative) and fine exhibitions of hair splitting, references to authorities, footnotes to footnotes will be made. In the Germanic tradition of scholarship the longest list of references will win the day. This makes it exceedingly difficult to state with any precision or clarity what constitutes the scientific method.

Nevertheless scientists do carry out experiments. They use their findings to develop theories and put them to the test with further experiment. Thus despite the problems of defining scientific method, there are *de facto* definitions in daily use in laboratories throughout the world. Philosophers of science, many of whom have never conducted an experiment in their lives, might well throw up their hands in horror at such a definition, but scientific method can be seen as essentially what scientists do. This is the working definition which I shall adopt in this chapter and to ensure its relevance to our aims and purposes, I will restrict myself to the methods used in psychology.

The scientific method

Nevertheless, given the problems of defining the scientific method and the not inconsiderable philosophical literature on its nature, I shall briefly examine some of the difficulties in this area, in order that my somewhat pragmatic, not to say behavioural, approach in defining the method, can be free of philosophic error.

Many working scientists, I think it is fair to say, follow the scientific logic of their work advocated by Karl Popper in *The Logic of Scientific Discovery*. The essence of this approach, to risk a gross simplification, is that in science, hypotheses must be expressed in a refutable form. Science is then concerned with the refutation of hypotheses. All scientific knowledge is thus provisional. At any point it may be refuted.

There is no doubt that, in psychology at least, a large number of experiments are carried out on this principle. Nevertheless the study of the history of science reveals that in many cases great discoveries and theories were not thus made. As Chalmers has pointed out (1978), Newton's gravitational theory appeared to be refuted by observations of the movements of the moon. However, it was not in fact rejected. In addition there is the philosophical difficulty that observations which are supposed to falsify theories or hypotheses are themselves theory dependent. Chalmers again supplies a nice astronomical example from the work of Copernicus whose theory implied that Venus should appear to change size during the year. Naked eye observation appeared to refute the claim. However, such naked eye observation has a theoretical supposition that the eye can estimate the size of small light sources. In fact, this theory assumption is wrong, as telescopic observation demonstrates. Finally, there is a further objection to the simple falsification approach – namely that, in fact, as the history of science demonstrates scientists are often happy to have their hypotheses confirmed.

This last point is important because even if a simple experiment is designed to put a hypothesis to the empirical test and the hypothesis is not rejected, most workers would regard that hypothesis as supported albeit tentatively. This is certainly the case in many psychological experiments. Here, however, an important distinction is drawn by philosophers of science. If a theory yields new and surprising hypotheses, especially when contra-intuitive, then confirmation is considered good support for theory. This is confirmation of bold conjectures. On the other hand, cautious conjectures that follow easily from the theory are only interesting if falsified. Now it is my contention that in psychology this approach has been grossly abused. Psychologists rarely go in for bold conjectures. Rather they use cautious conjectures and regard the theory as confirmed if they are supported. This is particularly true of the users of cognitive models described in the next chapter.

Because of these problems with the notion of refutability, even if the confirmation of novel hypotheses is allowed, some philosophers of science have argued that the scientific method is far more complex, involving whole programmes of work as discussed by Lakatos and (what has become very popular and current jargon in psychology) paradigms, as discussed by Kuhn (1975). Now I do not want to say much about these approaches to the notion of science because they are, with one exception, not relevant to my book which is concerned with the actual psychological findings that have emerged from experimental psychology and each experiment, whether in a programme or not, itself is usually designed according to the principles discussed by Popper.

The one exception concerns Kuhn's study of the progress of science and the work of scientists. According to Kuhn scientists usually work within a paradigm. Although hard to pin down, a paradigm may be considered to be a set of rules and theoretical assumptions which underlie the particular science. In its time Newtonian physics was a paradigm which gave a framework for physicists to carry out experiments and construct theories. If gradually findings emerge which demonstrate that the paradigm is unsatisfactory then there is scientific crisis until another paradigm emerges, and thus slowly does science change.

The relevance to my book of this conception of the scientific method is this. According to Kuhn scientists must be uncritical of the paradigms in which they work. Only thus can scientists carry out the laborious and detailed studies necessary to explicate the paradigm. Real science is distinguished from immature science by this one fact – the possession of a clear, accepted paradigm. Now in psychology most of the work is of the detailed kind, as if there were an accepted paradigm. Yet as I have already shown this is by no means the case. In fact, there are various models of psychology, all of which involve different paradigms. Furthermore, as I show throughout this book it is the uncritical acceptance of what are manifestly absurd paradigms and the refusal to examine them or consider a paradigm that is adequate for the nature of man that is at the root of the failure of experimental psychology.

Thus, in brief, although I realize that the Popperian falsification approach to the scientific method is flawed, because that is essentially the method of the working scientist in psychology (as distinct from the philosopher of science), I implicitly adopt it as the scientific method.

Scientific theories depend upon three elements: the first of these are the observations. These must be precise, quantified, replicable, and made under controlled conditions so that the role of other extraneous variables can be ruled out. In many of the natural sciences, observations can be made with prodigious accuracy, measures of electrical output, temperature, pressure, or amplitude, say, of wave forms.

As applied to psychology it means that the original data must be quantified hence the use of psychological tests. If observations of actual behaviour are made, then it is essential that there be high agreement among different observers, and that if the observations were to be made again at a later date then there should be little disagreement between the two sets of data.

The second element in the scientific process is the construct. Each construct must be operational. This means that it must have some clear and easily identified and agreed upon method of measuring or observing it. In psychology many of the constructs used fail to reach these operational criteria. A clear example is one of mental energy. This is a construct that enters into many accounts of human behaviour. Yet even to begin to measure it and thus operationalize it has so far defied psychologists.

The last of the three fundamental bases of the scientific method in psychology concerns the hypotheses which must be stated in a refutable form. This stems from the logical positivist approach to meaning. It is claimed by adherents to the scientific method that only thus is scientific progress brought about. If theories are not refutable they are never discarded. In this formulation, of course, all science is tentative, regarded as correct until it is shown to be wrong.

One notable aspect of the method is the emphasis on falsifiability and disconfirmation rather than confirmation. This is particularly relevant to such psychological theories as are rooted in clinical observation. Psychoanalysis is a particularly good example of how misleading confirmatory (rather than falsifying) evidence for hypothesis can be. Thus in the course of their practices most analysts from time to time come across supporting evidence for various Freudian hypotheses. This gives them, by such confirming instances and those of their colleagues, confidence in their theoretical position. Yet, alas, as a moment's reflection shows, this will not do. A hypothesis that swans are white can never be proven by seeing white swans, no matter how many. One black swan falsifies the hypothesis.

Such then is the scientific method as generally applied in experimental psychology. Rigorous, precise observation and quantification; constructs defined clearly and operationalized by good measure; control of all variables by experimental designs and above all clear statements of hypotheses put into a reputable form. The more experimental work conforms to these canons, the more scientific it is.

Reasons for using the scientific method

Having described the scientific method, *vis-à-vis* psychology, I will now examine the reasons for its use. This is necessary since, despite my contention that it has led to the valueless pursuit of trivia, its adherents must think otherwise and it has to be admitted that they are in the majority. Indeed, only outside experimental psychology, among the practitioners, is any voice raised against this scientific imperialism.

The first and most direct argument which is used to support the use of the scientific method in psychology is that only in this way was progress made in the great natural sciences – physics and chemistry. Before the scientific method belief in authorities, even those as great as Aristotle, had proved useless. Hence if progress is to be made in psychology, the argument runs, these same scientific methods must be used. Implicit in this argument is the assumption that science is the only way to knowledge.

The science of psychology, first practised in something like this form in Germany, is about a century old. Thus one scientific test of the claim that only scientific psychology can lead to knowledge is to see to what extent there is an agreed corpus of knowledge stemming from the utilization of this method.

The first curious and alarming point to note is that there is no agreement. There is no extensive canon of psychological findings which can be taken as read. For example a well-known textbook of personality – a standard text for undergraduates throughout the English speaking world – is forced to say that personality cannot be easily defined because there are as many theories as personality psychologists. Furthermore, this is true of virtually all branches of the subject. Indeed the scientific method judged by its own criteria of falsifiability has clearly failed to produce the goods. I shall take two examples to illustrate this failure. Is intelligence largely inherited or environmentally determined? Reputable psychologists claim heritability indices ranging from 75 per cent to 0 per cent. What are the causes of schizophrenia? Answers vary from childhood trauma arising from contradictory messages from parents about feelings of affection and hate, to a predisposition which when confronted with psychological difficulties leads on to schizophrenia, to a hypothesis claiming that it is largely genetic, arising from biochemical imbalances in the brain. Yet other workers deny the existence of the condition at all and claim that what is thought of as schizophrenia consists of symptoms which are naturally explicable in terms of the patient's life. Here clearly the scientific method has failed, as it has in my first example. Yet both these topics have been heavily researched.

Of course the fact that two important topics have not been explicated by the scientific method casts considerable doubt on its efficacy but the worshippers at the feet of science, as with many religious fanatics, are not discouraged by the brute facts of reality. Give us time, give us time, and all will be well. These subjects are peculiarly complex, perhaps too broad for solution. The mills of science grind slowly and grind exceedingly small. So runs the counter claim. It is naïve to expect answers to these questions, but to other more apposite ones, the scientific method yields results which can be put together to build up, to elucidate these wider issues. I shall now examine this argument, as it is explicated by Cattell (1981).

R. B. Cattell, who is certainly one of the most prolific and original of scientific psychologists and has for fifty years carried the torch of science aloft wrote in his final testament

Literary studies of personality help us to understand other personalities through our own experiences and introspections. The scientific study of personality seeks to understand personality as one would the mechanism of a watch, the chemistry of the life processes in a mammal or the spectrum of a remote star. That is to say it aims at objective insights; at the capacity to predict and control what will happen next; and at the establishment of scientific laws of a perfectly general nature.

Three other brief quotations from this lucid description and rationale of the scientific method will be useful. 'Psychology has been slow to realise what older sciences have learned, namely that progress in laws and principles begins only after measurement and description – taxonomy as it is broadly defined – have reached exact levels.' The second point is also highly relevant: 'the immature student begins by asking enormous questions and developing elaborate explanatory theories: but the mature investigator realises that we must describe thoroughly before we can begin to explain.' The third quotation is important in understanding another aspect of scientific psychology which is baffling to the uninitiated. 'I shall use technical terms going beyond the popular language of, say, novelists and some "humanistic" psychologists. As mediaeval science and physics have long known, nothing but confusion results from mixing popular words with strictly defined terms. So readers should not express surprise if new ideas require him or her to learn a new vocabulary.'

Problems with the scientific method

In my opinion Cattell's scientific credo, as stated above, contains within it all the reasons for the failure of scientific psychology to yield results of any value. However before I demonstrate this point, I must make it clear that these strictures are not aimed personally at Cattell. I have worked with Cattell on our book *The Scientific Study of Personality and Motivation* and I believe that he has used the scientific method about as well as it can be in psychology, and that he has attempted to avoid the trivial. However this credo can be and usually is grossly misinterpreted in the hands of Grub Street scientists.

The first point to note is that the scientific method is by implication held to be superior to the literary, 'our own experiences and introspections' are denigrated, inferior to the objectivity of science. However there is a certain irony in this point because actually our own experiences are the only things we can know about with any confidence. If I feel sad, I do so and I am not mistaken. To thus ignore experience is odd.

Another important point is the argument that we want to understand personality as we would the mechanism of a watch. This analogy is by no means a good one. First there is no disagreement as to what is a watch or not. If I pick up a watch, no one is going to say that it is not a watch. The worst that could be done is that someone else call it a clock. However there would be no disagreement as to whether it was a complete object or not. This is not so with personality. Personality is only a construct, it has no independent existence beyond the mind that conceived it. In that sense the mechanisms are part of the conception and also have no existence independent of it. Thus whatever studying objectively the processes of personality may mean, it certainly is quite unlike studying the finite mechanisms of a watch. A similar objection applies to Cattell's other examples. A mammal is a definite organism – its life processes are finite, chemical, electrical events. Of course objective study of these is perfectly possible and infinitely superior to endless speculation about the nature of blood or the balance of the aqueous humours of the body.

Notice that there is no analogous argument from the mammal to personality. There can be no descent into a physiological universe of discourse. Of course it is possible to study the human physiology by the scientific method, but this is not studying personality or psychology. Even if physiology is studied alongside behaviour it adds nothing to our understanding of psychology. Suppose that cortical cells A and B always fired when I saw red and at no other time. What does this tell us about my experience of red? Indeed it is banal because it goes without saying that there must be neural biochemical or electrical changes underlying experience, for there can be no other.

Similarly, to understand the spectrum of a remote star is the study of a phenomenon which can be verified in a number of ways, and is not only a concept within the head of the investigator. In other words this credo for the scientific method in psychology, on analysis, has revealed one of the major weaknesses of the whole approach which is probably so serious as to render it worthless on its own. It is true that scientific method has worked well in engineering, biology and astronomy but the human psyche is not an essentially mechanical object. The human brain is susceptible to much study but the mind belongs to a different universe of discourse where methods such as these do not seem to apply. Parenthetically a much more modern scientific approach than that of Cattell is of course that of computational models and artificial intelligence. However the same logical error obtains – this time that the mind is like a computer. This is a more subtle distortion and I shall deal with the evils of computational psychology in a separate chapter.

In brief, therefore it is clear that the scientific method is unsuited to psychology because the subject matter of psychology is conceptually different from that of the classical sciences for which the method was developed. This is a fundamental problem of the scientific method in psychology.

However Cattell's credo reveals several other features of the scientific method which have led to its failure in psychology. These are not fundamental errors or weaknesses but rather aspects of the method which when taken up by scientists of modest ability and imagination inevitably lead to sterile and trivial research, work which is, unfortunately, reinforced, as I will show, by the society and institutions in which modern scientists are employed.

Since the full quotations have already been given in the credo, I shall paraphrase the points here. First there is the importance given to exact measurement, description and taxonomy. The second point emphasizes the immaturity of asking broad questions and the necessity for, in the first place, minute description. The third point emphasizes the need for a new, precise, vocabulary, undefiled by the usage of the common man.

These three tenets have been abused in experimental psychology because it seems to be the case that if a study has exact measurement, asks a minute question and employs long neologisms, it is regarded as acceptable. Thus even if the three points of the credo were true this would constitute a monstrous logical error. This is the fallacy of the occluded middle. If a study is scientific it must contain precise measurement. From this it does not follow that all studies with precise measurement are scientific, and the same argument applies to the other points.

I will now consider these in a little more detail, which will reveal the nature and implications of this logical flaw. I fully agree that precise measurement is important. The banal nature of this claim is surely indicated by its opposite. Anybody who argued that imprecise measurement was preferable to precise would rightly be considered mad, although to argue that no measurement is best is a different point. However the demand for precision has led empirical psychologists to choose variables *because they can be so measured* and not for reasons of theoretical psychology. This has led to research into trivial issues. A common point that journal editors and referees are asked to comment upon is the precision of the measurement. In the language of psychometrics are the tests reliable and valid? Thus one criterion for even beginning a piece of research is whether or not the variable can be precisely measured. Unfortunately many human characteristics and feelings which are important to most people are not thus amenable to measurement and hence are neglected.

A measurement of precision of a test is its reliability which essentially indicates its internal coherence and freedom from random errors of measurement. A reliability coefficient of 0 demonstrates that the test is no more than a collection of unconnected items. The closer the index approaches 1, the more precise it is. O. K. Buros publishes every five years a handbook of published tests in psychology, entitled *Mental Measurements Year Book*, of which there are now several thousands. Many of them are reliable but a glance at the titles strongly supports my contention that precision has overruled psychological significance.

Athletic motivation inventory, consumer rights and responsibilities test, consumer competences test, getting along (self-acceptance, acceptance by others, facing reality), attitudes to disabled persons, adolescent alienation index, dictation test, life goals evaluation schedule, and so it goes. What has happened is that psychologists have thought of a variable, written items which are apparently relevant to it, and eliminated those that are not highly correlated with each other – thus producing a reliable measure. Given say a measure of getting along, a number of studies can be developed. Age differences in getting along; sex differences in getting along; getting along with children of the same and different sex; social class differences in getting along; educational attainment and getting along; intelligence and getting along; getting along in rural and urban children; factors influencing failure to get along; the relation of getting along to: introversion; anxiety;

obsessionality; racial differences in getting along. Similar studies could be carried out using the dictation test: ability in dictation and: intelligence; verbal ability; verbal ability with intelligence held constant; intelligence with verbal ability held constant.

Studies of this type which fill journals and allow awards of numerous research degrees throughout the English speaking world, also fulfil the second criterion, namely that research (of mature investigators) be concerned with small answerable questions. I will consider this argument with some care because it is frequently used to support research which on any other grounds would be considered absurd. First of all it is banal to argue that research should be concerned with answerable questions. It is, by definition, pointless to attempt to find answers to questions which cannot be answered. However this requires judgement and with imagination and flair an investigator could easily manage to put to the operational test an idea that defeated the majority of his colleagues. Indeed, it has been pointed out by Grünbaum in his discussion of the notion of falsifiability in the scientific method that there is no other meaning to the statement that X is unfalsifiable than that the speaker cannot think of a way of so doing. Thus the easy, safe way to carry out experiments is to pick easy questions with reliable tests (thus meeting the first two criteria) and all will be well.

There is a further issue which concerns the choice of question to be investigated. Some large questions can be broken down into small points which can then be subjected to experimental scrutiny. The results can then be synthesized into a meaningful whole. But many small researches can never be used to form any bricks or building blocks for theories. After all the number of possible questions is infinite and if those are selected simply because they are small in scope and involve variables which are easy to measure there is no reason why they should be useful for theoretical synthesis.

The final point concerns neologisms. It is perfectly true that words with popular meaning are difficult to use with scientific precision on account of their connotations and that within natural language, a certain freedom of play is possible. However the mention of neologisms for their own sake and the use of jargon is often not for the sake of precision but for camouflage – the banality of the ideas in normal language. I take as my example a well-known model in social psychology – the Fishbein Model.

This is designed to predict an individual's intention to perform a behaviour. According to this model the strength of one's intentions to perform a behaviour is a function of two factors (a) beliefs about the consequences or outcomes of performing the behaviour and the evaluation of those consequences and (b) subjective normative belief about what others think the actor should do and the actor's motivation to comply with those beliefs.

(Pagel and Davidson, 1984)

So far so good, I think nobody would feel surprised if he were told that people's intentions are influenced by what they think will happen if they do or do not do whatever they intend, and other's opinions of these actions. It would appear so obvious that the designation 'model' is somewhat pompous. However, Fishbein goes well beyond this trite formulation because this is turned not simply into neologisms but into the sacred language of science, the mystic script known only to those few who have undergone the dreaded rites of initiation. I mean, of course, mathematics. This becomes

$$B \cong B1 \left(\sum_{i=1}^{n} bi\, ei \right) W_1 + \left(\sum_{J=1}^{m} nbj\, mcj \right) W_2$$

where B is overt behaviour, $B1$ is the intention to perform the behaviour, bi is the belief that performing the behaviour will lead to consequence; ei is the evaluation of consequence i, nbj is the perceived expectation of referent group or individual J, mcj is the motivation to comply with J, n is the number of salient consequences, m is the number of salient normative beliefs and W_1 and W_2 are empirically determined regression weights.

Thus Fishbein converts two simple beliefs into a scientific model. All the measurements can be done on seven-point rating scales. For me this is difficult to take seriously. There is even a logical problem in the model which, given its context, is perhaps hardly worthy of comment. However there is no conceptual distinction between the consequences of behaviour, and what people think of it, which has to be taken into account. It is only a consequence of doing it that people's belief about it become salient. My argument is that a set of ideas is no better for being couched in an abstruse language. What counts is the quality of the idea in the first place.

In summary, therefore, I argue that even if good science demands precise quantification, narrow concepts and accurate expression, it by no means follows logically that work possessing these characteristics is good science. In other words good science has yet further characteristics beyond these. In fact, as my first chapter made clear, the weakness of experimental psychology lies in its disjunction from important questions. This disjunction arises in part, as I have demonstrated in this chapter, from the scientific credo itself. A method has been adopted which was suited to subject matter in a materialistic universe of discourse but was not so appropriate for psychological constructs.

If all my arguments are accepted, and it seems to me an over-whelming case, then we are left with a conundrum. Why do experimental psychologists continue with their work? I shall examine the reasons for the continuation of what appears so unpromising a tradition because they reveal why any hope of change is so remote and why an entirely new approach is both necessary and so hard to bring about.

Why psychologists continue to use the scientific method

An important element in the maintenance of the scientific method in psychology, almost in the face of evidence, is the prestige attached to science in the west and in technologically advanced societies. The white-coated scientist in his laboratory eerily lit by the constant flicker of LED's and computer screens amidst the manic clutter of printers is a symbol of the power of science and its hierophants, but not unlike the white-robed druids clustered around the standing stones of Stonehenge beneath a morning sun. Not for nothing, perhaps, the great monoliths are now thought to be a kind of celestial calendar – placed with wonderful precision to indicate the motion of the stars.

In British universities pure science is held in greater esteem by far than engineering or other applied science and attracts candidates with the best possible qualifications, even though prospects for employment are now less favourable. Psychologists, in Don Bannister's phrase, are eager to join the Science Club. This pressure from the prestige of science, to keep psychology scientific, is further reinforced by the evil repute of the social sciences leading indeed to the change of title of the SSRC to ESRC – Economic and Social Research Council.

A second powerful influence springs from the character of those who take up experimental psychology. People in touch with their own feelings would hardly be attracted by a discipline which avowedly, in some of its emanations, denies the notion of feelings or at least minimizes their importance. Thus behaviourism, which argues that there is no need to study thought and feelings as these are only inferred from overt behaviour and are at best mere epiphenomena of conditioned responses, inevitably attracts those who want to deny their feelings. Experimental psychology, in psychoanalytic terms, allows many defences against emotions to be put into operation. Denial: there are no feelings, they are mere epiphenomena; reaction-formation: there are feelings but they are of no consequence in understanding human behaviour; intellectualization: feelings are studied even if they are denied. In some way they enter the discourse of the investigations. Displacement is easily observed. This results in putting enormous effort into the study of trivial safe subjects. In brief it is highly likely that those who are attracted by experimental psychology are so attracted because it minimizes the force of feelings and emotions and is concerned with their control by their reduction to mathematical formulae or regression weights – all manageable by the intellect. Figure 2.1 indicates how attractive such an approach must be to those whose emotions are a cause of anxiety. 'Oh tell me where is fancy bred/In the heart or in the head?' to quote Shakespeare's Jacques in As You Like It.

Thus I argue that the type of people who are attracted into experimental psychology make it inevitable that the subject remains as mathematical and precise as it is possible to make it and hence will eschew all those topics which do not easily submit themselves to such treatment and especially those whose emotional nature is likely to create anxiety. Certainly what empirical work there is on the nature of research scientists in all disciplines including psychology shows them to be cold and aloof, people who like working alone, wrapped up in their own ideas. Indeed they are neurotic introverts, a finding which fits the claims which I have made about their emotional defences.

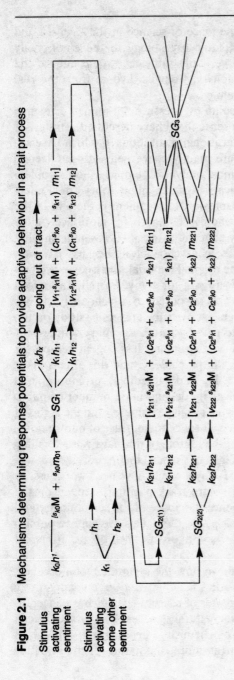

Figure 2.1 Mechanisms determining response potentials to provide adaptive behaviour in a trait process

Source: Cattell (1981)

These two arguments, the place of science in the *Zeitgeist* and the attractiveness of a scientific psychology to the emotionally deprived or repressed are certainly sufficient to account for the triviality of much of psychology, from its divorce from the real questions of human psychology.

There is yet another point of pressure to render academic psychology scientific in the sense that I have described. This arises from the nature of the educational institutions in which psychologists work. Universities are mainly concerned with intellectual matters, and there is almost universal emphasis on problem solving and learning. Education of the mind splits off intellect and emotion. Objective dispassionate argument is the aim of the university educator. Scientific psychology is far more acceptable in the context of university education. Indeed it is significant that no university offers courses in psychoanalysis because it is not objective but subjective; the original material, the free association of patients, cannot be drawn upon for study. Farrell, an Oxford philosopher, by no means ill disposed to psychoanalysis, has argued that it is not a suitable subject for university study on the grounds that students could never scrutinize primary sources.

There is a further more venial but no less cogent reason for the proliferation of triviality in psychology, and this affects other subjects as well. Regrettably, and incredibly, promotion and career prospects in the university depend upon number of publications. In one university, which shall be nameless, on the forms of application for a lectureship was space to put titles of publications, including page numbers. At the bottom of this page was a heading 'Total Number of Pages'. Einstein's special theory of relativity was a one-page note in *Nature*. Today it would have been worthless. In the USA too salaries and tenure track positions depend on the number of publications. Hence the abuse of the scientific method which allows easy and quick publication. This pressure to publish is responsible in part for some of the ills of experimental psychology.

In this chapter I have shown how the scientific method is not, as defined by one of the world's leading practitioners, apparently well suited to the subject matter of psychology which is conceptually different from that of the natural sciences. Of course man can be described in terms of biochemistry, or anatomy, but this is clearly not psychology. Furthermore, the nature of the scientific method, with its emphasis on precision and limitations to the questions asked, encourages work which is essentially trivial but correct and technically faultless. The production of such work, I have argued, is facilitated in the current scientific *Zeitgeist*, by the kind of people who are attracted to experimental psychology and by the institutions in which they work.

All these arguments account for the use and failure of the scientific method in general and for the main problem, the disjunction of experimental psychology and human psychology, as it is widely conceived by non-psychologists.

However psychologists can still raise objections to these points. In general, though there may be some force in the arguments, my examples were slanted to suit them. Personality is a notoriously slippery topic which has shown itself difficult to master by scientific procedures. In other fields, however, better defined and conceptualized with greater clarity, experimental psychology has been effective, not just in elucidating trivia, but in building up a sound body of empirical knowledge. The great fields of psychology, perception, learning, cognitive psychology, for example, are not thus empty.

Rationale for the rest of the book

In the next chapters, I intend to examine some of the main fields of psychology in order to scrutinize what experimental psychology has achieved and to evaluate its potential. As I pointed out in the first chapter, to some extent the kind of psychology that is done depends upon one's views of man and many of the main areas of psychology reflected such views either explicitly or implicitly. In fact, the fields I have chosen to examine are not only important parts of experimental psychology but represent some of the most influential viewpoints concerning the nature of man.

Thus in the next chapter I examine cognitive psychology. Modern cognitive psychology is underpinned by one of the most recent psychological metaphors – man the computer, the information processor, the Turing Machine. In addition it reflects, I suspect, the old eighteenth-century viewpoint of man as rational animal – *cogito ergo sum*. It is obvious given these implicit assumptions that in this work the role of feelings and emotions would be minimized.

In Chapter 4 I scrutinize psychometrics. This represents in its modern form trait psychology and the genetic viewpoint – man as a collection of traits some learned in the main, others largely heritable. With such assumptions the factor analytic measurement approach is naturally fitting. Here people are seen as essentially static and unchanging, all ranked along psychological dimensions, a world of elites and also rans.

In Chapter 5 I examine some important aspects of social psychology which was characterized as an attempt to avoid the errors, obvious in the traditional experimental psychological laboratory, of investigating behaviour without reference to its social context. This work reflects a view of man as a social animal. It is, therefore, an important field.

In Chapter 6 I investigate the work that explicitly derives from the model of man the computer. This, of course, is the work in artificial intelligence, machine perception and cognitive science. This is currently the most rigorous and innovative field in psychology and again, as might be expected from the underlying model, this approach is not at ease with feelings and emotions.

In Chapter 7 I examine animal psychology. First I investigate the claims of sociobiology. This clearly sees man as an animal, who aims, as do all organisms, to preserve his genes. The viability of the work stemming from this viewpoint to understand the richness and depths of human feelings is examined. I then turn to Skinnerian behaviourism which sees behaviour simply as the result of reinforcement. The poverty and implausibility of this viewpoint, brilliantly though it is advocated, becomes clear on scrutiny. Finally in this chapter I look at ethology. Thus the three great psychological traditions stemming from the notion of man the animal are discussed.

In the final chapter, in the light of the conclusions which I have drawn concerning these branches of psychology, I attempt to suggest how things may be improved, how psychology can deal rigorously with the problems that are truly germane to man. This then is the rationale to the topics which I have examined in this book; they represent important areas of experimental psychology and reflect most of the influential views on the nature of man.

One further point needs to be made concerning the content of these chapters. This is the matter of the selection of topics. It is clearly impossible for me to cover all these fields in their entirety.

In selecting topics and finding them flawed or failing to deal with important issues, opponents of my thesis, lovers of experimental psychology as it is (yes there are such, alas, in the academic world) not as it might be, can always argue that I deliberately selected weak or absurd topics; that every subject has its foibles and its apparently weak research; that in reality there are noble and fine researches that I have deliberately or through ignorance disregarded. That is the defence and that was the argument against my Inaugural Lecture on this theme in Exeter in 1986. Unfortunately it will not do. In cognitive psychology and social psychology, I deliberately did not select the topics myself. Instead I chose those regarded as most important in two textbooks, one by Michael Eysenck, the other by my colleague, Richard Eiser, textbooks which are considered excellent summaries of the field. These are topics which Eysenck and Eiser consider to be significant aspects of their subjects. If such topics *are* trivial, then the whole field must be so as well.

In the case of cognitive science, I took papers from a special issue of *Cognitive Science* which was designed to explicate the state of the art in the field. In addition, I examined the work of Marr on machine perception which is considered to be seminal in cognitive science. As regards animal psychology, a study of Skinner's work, the work of Wilson in sociobiology and Hinde in ethology cannot be argued to be lighting on absurd or trivial examples.

Attractive and logically always possible as this counter argument is, it is clearly wrong. My selection of fields and the topics within them does reflect experimental psychology. Yet regrettably as I shall show, experimental psychology is found to be wanting, regrettably because for more than one hundred years so much time and energy has been put into it and been ineluctably wasted.

Chapter three

The discoveries of cognitive psychology: Models of memory. Are they of any value?

In this chapter, I intend to examine some of the main findings from cognitive psychology, in order to test my claim that, as I argued in the first two chapters, experimental psychology must ultimately end up with the trivial and fail to engage with what is of importance to most human beings.

Michael Eysenck in 1984 produced an excellent and well-balanced summary of recent work in cognitive psychology and I have used this as a basis for my discussion, although my views are totally different from his.

Definition of cognitive psychology

Cognitive psychology, defined here as the study of the processes and mechanisms underlying human cognition, has become according to Eysenck almost synonymous with experimental psychology. Hence it is fitting to begin the more detailed analysis with this branch of psychology.

Actually cognitive psychology enters into very many quite disparate fields ranging from social psychology (which I shall deal with in a separate chapter), memory, imagery, artificial intelligence, to language and thought just for example. However I intend to pick out some of what are regarded as the most powerful of the findings of cognitive psychology in the field of memory rather than take examples from every branch of this subject.

First, I want to scrutinize the definition offered by Eysenck – 'cognitive psychology is concerned with the *processes and mechanisms underlying* cognition'. It will be recalled that I discussed, in Chapter 2, Cattell's scientific credo that we lay bare the 'structure of personality like the mechanism of a watch'. I pointed out that this analogy was spurious because the mechanisms and processes of personality lay within a universe of discourse different (that is, not materialistic) from those of a watch. It is quite clear that the mechanisms and processes of cognition are within this same psychological universe of discourse such that objective, scientific methods may not suit them well. In this field, my general objection to the scientific method appears to hold. Of course, it is possible to study the anatomy and biochemistry of cognition but this is clearly physiology not psychology, and such investigations will not be discussed in this book. For this work the scientific method may well be excellent.

Models of human memory: Baddeley's model

I will now turn to a branch of cognitive psychology which has been extensively worked over a number of years – the construction of models of human memory. There has been a variety of models which have been elaborated and developed to fit experimental findings but I shall scrutinize a recent version which seems to be still acceptable – Baddeley's model of working memory. Working memory has three components: first, a central executive which is modality-free like a pure attentional system, and which possesses two slave components. Then there is the articulatory loop in which information is phonemically encoded, and of which the capacity is determined by temporal duration. The third component is the visual-spatial memory which relies on spatial coding. More recently further assumptions have had to be introduced, including a distinction between articulatory coding and acoustic coding and an input register in which a panel representation of recent words is stored – essential for comprehension.

This model of how material is encoded in and retrieved from memory is designed to account for the experimental findings in the study of human memory. It is able to accommodate the fact that verbal rehearsal plays a smaller role than might be thought in memory, and that other kinds of rehearsal are equally effective. Furthermore, it has been shown that the main component of the system is active in tasks (involving memory) beyond simple memorizing such as mental arithmetic (which also involves the articulatory loop) verbal reasoning and comprehension.

This model is also able to account for some of the more detailed findings of cognitive research into memory. For example, that short-term memory is much influenced by verbal coding, such that phonemically similar items even if visually presented are much less well recalled; word length is also an influential factor. Similarly, it fits the fact that uttering something between items to be learned lessens recall and cancels out the other effects mediated by the articulatory loop. The recency effect in recall (e.g. the end of a list is better recalled than the rest) is also accounted for by the input register of the model. A further justification for the model comes from the fact that if two tasks, which putatively use different components of the model, are presented together, then there is no interference between them in learning.

As Eysenck demonstrates there has been a variety of experimental efforts to show how this model is involved in reading. For example, the articulatory loop can be suppressed and does not affect the comprehension of sentences or judging whether they be true or false. However in other experiments memory for sentences was affected. Thus sometimes the loop is used, though sometimes not, in reading, perhaps when other components of the system are overloaded, as when the material is highly complex. Experiments show that suppression of the articulatory loop does not affect memory for thematic material (as distinct from unrelated sentences). This is taken to indicate that top-down processing is important in reading, top-down meaning affected by what a subject already brings to the problem (prior knowledge, experience and so on). This contrasts with bottom-up processing which refers to what is immediately affected by the input. There is further evidence from studies of this kind that the 'inner ear' (acoustic coding) is influential. Thus when subjects had to clarify visually presented nonsense words as sounding similar or not to real words, burd would be an example, or bizen, such a task was not affected by suppression of the loop but subjects according to their introspective reports appeared to use such codes.

There are several points which I think should be made about this model of working memory. The first one questions the point and purpose of the model. It accounts for certain observations in memory experiments, but we already know these. So what is added by this model? Perhaps the argument might be that of Cattell's credo – detailed description is necessary for scientific understanding. However how does this model tell us more than the experimental results? Even if results could be predicted from it they would be of the same narrow kind as the data it encapsulates. This model seems nothing more than a neat descriptive account of the experimental findings. I contend that there is nothing else for which it can be used.

Eysenck tries to argue that it is useful for the study of reading. However if the articulatory loop is or is not used or if an acoustic code is used, what does this tell us that would affect the teaching of reading either to children or adults? Even here the model does nothing but describe the experimental findings.

Why, therefore, is the working model of memory still a viable model tested and examined in experimental psychology? I can only conclude, and I do not intend this cynically, that it reflects the institution of science in the United Kingdom. Baddeley is one of our most distinguished cognitive psychologists, heading perhaps the most prestigious research unit in the country, with a large number of grants for students. To test the Baddeley model in different conditions and with different materials and with different subjects, to compare it with other similarly conceived models, is a simple task for the experimentally competent, guaranteed to produce faultless yet entirely trivial papers. The model is a generator of research projects, so it must be good.

Ecological validity

There is a further difficulty with the experimental work which forms the basis of this model and which the model is designed to encapsulate. This is called by those psychologists who dare even to criticize mildly so definitive a model, ecological validity. In English this questions whether the experiments which were performed in the laboratory bear any relation to any other kind of behaviour at all except these and similar experiments. If they do not, then, of course, any kind of generalization is quite absurd.

I shall exemplify these data so that readers may judge to what extent this difficulty intrudes on standard interpretations of the results. In some experiments subjects are presented with phrases to be categorized as meaningful or not meaningful. Some groups of words can be meaningful, others can be nonsense but sound meaningful, some can simply be and sound meaningless. Examples of the latter two: Save the Whale, fly the plain, hug the lamb, flen a champon. Reaction times to the different groups of words are compared. From data such as these, phonemic coding is supposed to occur in reading. However the task of categorizing groups of words as meaningful or not is not really like reading. Certainly it involves reading but most people read for pleasure or to gain information. Furthermore, reading has serious emotional connotations on occasion, as for example when reading pornography, a letter informing you that your PhD thesis has been turned down, or that your lover is pregnant or no longer your lover, or that you have an overdraft of £2,000, or that your holiday in China is now completely washed out, or that the rear disc of your car, which you had hoped to remove, can never be removed. Furthermore, most adults, when reading books especially, read large chunks at a time.

Other writers have commented upon the absurdity of some of the task requirements in experiments of this type. In one experiment, for example, reported by Eysenck, subjects have to decide whether 'canaries have wings' is true or false and similarly for 'canaries have gills'. Consider real reading, compare the Shakespearean sonnet

Like as the waves move towards the pebbled shore
so do our minutes hasten to their end

With experimental pairs of words as for example:

Canaries have wings.   True false
Canaries have gills.   True false

Is burd real? Yes No
Is bizen real? Yes No

Save the whale and fly the plain.
Hug the lamb and flen a champon.

In summary I cannot see what Baddeley's working model of memory can add to knowledge. It exemplifies to perfection my argument that experimental psychology is lost in the slough of trivia and with models of this kind the only progress is downward ever deeper. One day, perhaps in a thousand years, it will be recovered perfectly preserved, an astonishing peat model revered by archaeologists of science, shown to an amazed public in its brown stained rags.

Although the working model of memory was devised to account for the differences in the ability to recall what we know and recognize, the latter being easier, psychologists have devoted considerable research time to elucidating this problem, which although small, could well lead to a fuller understanding of human memory; and it is certainly true, from the viewpoint of psychology which I have adopted in this book, that memory is an important psychological process. After all it is the case that the infant, trailing clouds of glory and immortality, enters the world knowing nothing, but in adulthood generally knows something, although he may well leave it in the state he entered alas, sans eyes, sans teeth, sans everything.

One reason for the work on recall and recognition is that psychologists wish to understand the basis of the phenomenon. Originally it was thought, as Eysenck argues, that strength of a memory trace would account for the fact that recognition was easier than recall. However this will not do because rare words are better recognized than common words. Thus their memory traces should be stronger, yet recall is not so good. Thus the simple relationship does not hold. More elaborate models are required.

Tulving's model

Tulving is one of the most diligent research workers in the field of recognition and recall (1983), and I want to examine his model to see whether it illuminates the problem and allows psychological insights that are relevant to anything beyond the laboratory experiments which it was developed to understand.

Tulving's model has two kinds of elements, those concerned with encoding and those with retrieval. Something is encoded forming a memory trace or engram, which may be modified by encoding other later material. In retrieval, according to this model ecphory is vital because ecphory utilizes retrieval cues and the recoded engram and then produces the recollective experience,

Figure 3.1   The general abstract processing system

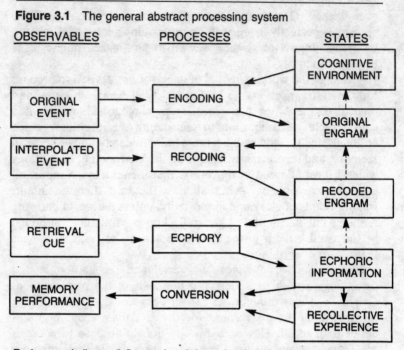

OBSERVABLES   PROCESSES   STATES

Each arrow indicates 'influences' or 'brings about', and broken arrows refer to effects that do not influence a current act of remembering, but may affect subsequent ones.

Source: Eysenck (1984)

the conscious awareness of ecphoric information. The process of conversion, utilizing this recollective experience or ecphoric information (which is below the level of awareness), allows overt behaviour. A feature of the conversion process is that recall and recognition have different thresholds. More ecphoric information is needed for recall than recognition because recall requires naming an event, while recognition requires only judgement of what is familiar. One other formulation is required for this model to work. The principle of encoding specificity is assumed; the probability of successful retrieval of the target item is a function of the overlap between the information present at retrieval and the information stored in memory.

First I shall make some general points about this model which seems largely descriptive if not actually tautologous. Consider first the meanings of recall and recognize. Recall, according to the

Oxford English Dictionary, means to bring back to the mind, or to remember some event. To recognize means literally to know again, to perceive to be identical with something previously known. Thus by definition more information is needed for the former than the latter. This is why there are two words in the language, to reflect this difference in performance. Thus the fact that the model shows that more information is needed for recall than recognition simply reflects the meaning of the words. All that the model does is suggest a system which allows for this fact. Notice the language Eysenck uses to describe the model. 'Recall requires naming an event, while recognition requires . . .' What is meant by 'requires'? Recall *is* naming the event, just as recognition *is* judging it to be similar. Again the specificity principle is banal. Successful retrieval from memory is a function of the overlap of information present at retrieval and information stored in memory. Suppose that retrieval was independent of information in the memory. This is senseless. Suppose it was independent of the information at time of retrieval. This too is simply contrary to experience. Thus the only value of the specificity principle is that it is a monotonically increasing function of the information overlap, but how is this information overlap to be measured? The model, in this view, simply posits a system which encapsulates the findings from the empirical study of the differences between recall and recognition. It seems unable to do more than this and nor do the hypothetical processes give rise to any insights or provide practical applications. Ecphory refers to the extraction of information from retrieval cues and engrams. There *must* be a process of this kind, given that we conceptualize memory as a coded store of some kind. Thus unless the ecphoric process can be accurately specified or otherwise delineated, even physiologically, the construct is of little interest.

In brief, the Tulving model is little more than a descriptive elaboration of the simple assumptions that almost all human beings have made about memory, namely that information is stored somewhere in the head and has to be retrieved. Indeed it would be possible to have a Hunting Model of Memory, where Beaters provided the cues, Pointers guided the way to the locations (Kennels) and Retrievers acquired the information. With a little elaboration – *Dachshunds* for the obscure bits of knowledge and Irish Wolfhounds to account for the phenomenal memnonist – the Hunting Model of Memory might take the academic road.

I have demonstrated that these two models of memory are elaborate descriptions of what is meant by memorizing which will account for the laboratory-based experimental observations but offer no insights or practical applications of any significance. In effect, they translate what was discovered experimentally into different terms. However both these models are concerned with the rather literal memorizing of bits of information, that aspect of memory called episodic, rather than with meaningful knowledge.

Meaningful knowledge, quite different from the word tests of episodic memory experiments – nonsense syllables, nonsense phrases, false statements and so on – is thought, by some psychologists, at least, to be stored in a different long-term memory, semantic memory, which nevertheless must be related in some way to the episodic memory. Meaningful knowledge, knowledge of the world, is of course, much more the memory of the real world. Indeed some of the criticisms of the memory models which I have already made were essentially of this kind. Episodic memory is, perhaps, an artefact of experimental psychology. Words bereft of their connotations and associations are rarely required for memory in real life. The sort of fact that requires the notion of semantic memory is, for example, the effortless ease with which we can reject the claim that vultures are translucent. This piece of information is unlikely to be stored in memory. Thus there must be some hierarchical arrangement of information in semantic memory such that inferences and deductions can be made virtually automatically.

It could therefore be the case, in principle, that my earlier strictures on the trival nature of memory studies apply only to the work on episodic memory. The work on meaningful, semantic memory, may, indeed bear on the important problems of psychology and here, at last, the chasm of reality and experiment may be bridged.

Semantic memory

One approach to understanding semantic memory was the activation model developed by Collins and Loftus – a network model. In this model knowledge is structured according to how related it is in semantic terms. How related one concept is to another is indicated by their linkages, for example, membership or not of superordinate categories is very important. If I read about a badger, a relevant node in the semantic memory is activated, and this spreads to neighbouring concepts – mammal, organism, perhaps. The spread of this activation depends upon how strongly 'badger' was activated, for example, it could be activated considerably by an interesting account of its habits or by an excellent nature film. Time too influences the spread, which lessens as time passes. In addition to this, sets of decision processes are built into the model. All the evidence from different paths of activation, from different links and the total strength are taken into account and the positive evidence is compared with the negative.

I shall take some examples similar to those used by Eysenck in his description of his model and then I want to discuss the claims made by Eysenck about the model, claims which are generally accepted in cognitive psychology. I shall demonstrate that these views do not stand rigorous scrutiny and that this network model is best abandoned.

Examples of these decision processes are: 'all mammals are badgers' is easily shown to be false by the activation of a counter example, weasel. If I ask myself the question 'is a badger a mammal?' the activation of connections badger and mustelid (the genus which includes weasels and badgers), and mustelid and mammal would be rapid. Similarly the evaluation of 'is a badger a bear?' is contradicted by linking badger to mustelid and mustelid to bear, which is mutually exclusive.

Now this activation model suffers from precisely the ills that beset the two other models which I have discussed. It simply states formally a set of procedures that will account for the differences observed in the experimental task of verifying whether a sentence is true or false. Even if it were agreed that knowledge was stored in this way it would tell you little about the nature of memory that was useful for any practical purpose or any further theoretical developments.

The failure of this model other than to encapsulate these simple experimental findings (which in real life may not hold if for example subjects lack the relevant information or have misinformation), is amply confirmed by the claim which Eysenck makes about it: 'This model has the advantage that it makes clear that the meaning of a word is substantially affected by the relationship of that word*s* [sic] and its associated concepts' (1984). As it stands (ignoring the false plural) this statement is nonsense. The concepts associated with a word should be the same, if semantic distance has a meaning. If that is the case, then the meaning of a word cannot be thus affected. If it is intended to mean that the associations which each individual makes regarding a word are different and these associations affect its meaning, thus there are differences in meaning of words among individuals, then this is, equally obviously, true. However such difference must be unimportant or else words would be incomprehensible to others and dialogue would be impossible. Furthermore, the examples of this structure given by Collins and Loftus are not of the kind that such individual differences would eliminate. What I take it to mean, is that meaning depends upon the associated concepts of a word, a proposition that badly needs a model to defend. Thus I would still argue that this network model is nothing more than a simple descriptive account of little more than commonsense psychology that does encapsulate some experimental evidence. I do not intend to say more about this model which has been superseded, to some extent, by computer models which I shall talk about in a later chapter.

Conclusions

I shall try to summarize the arguments and evaluate the scientific utility of these three models of memory. As I see it they are simply descriptive models which will account for the narrow experimental observations for which they were intended. As I have shown these models are not capable of yielding insights into wider theoretical issues or practical problems. In many cases, it appears, they state in detail what is implied by the actual terms.

As I argued in my analysis of the credo such detailed description is valuable in a study of objects, as in many sciences, but is not useful in the study of concepts where such description is, in the real sense of the term, fantastical. To describe a process in detail when the detail gives no advantage except in descriptive terms seems pointless. This is quite unlike the watch, for example, where the revelation of the detail can be linked to function. The detail of constructs can never be so convincing, because other interpretations are usually possible.

The construction of detailed models to account for experimental data means that they are constantly changing to accommodate new findings and in addition are limited to this narrow data-base. It virtually ensures that the work will be trivial.

I am, therefore, forced to conclude that the study of these models and other similar work is the transmutation of experimental psychology from science to hermeneutics. If the research practitioners would admit that their work was concerned with a world of models of human memory and bore reference only to itself and impinged upon reality by an occasional serendipity then we could treat it on its merits – which, as I have shown, are not considerable. If I want hermeneutics give me a system of some formal elegance and power, not the ponderous banality of ecphory.

Chapter four

Psychometrics: Measuring the soul or rendering it to ashes?

Psychometrics is the branch of psychology concerned with psychological testing and its associated statistical techniques. It was one of the few parts of psychology that originated and were developed in Great Britain, although now there are few researchers in this field, and I am the only Professor of Psychometrics in Great Britain.

The development of psychometrics

Psychometrics, in something like its current form, has been going for about fifty years and in this chapter I shall evaluate its main findings with reference to my claim that experimental scientific psychology by its insistence on precision and vigour has concentrated upon the trivial.

Before I can do this, I need to say something about the place of psychometrics within experimental psychology. This is not a piece of academic quibbling, for its own sake, but it is necessary for understanding what psychometrics has achieved, exactly as, in previous chapters, we saw how much apparently fruitless experimental psychology was kept going by the institutionalization of science within the university system both here and in the United States of America. In addition I must say something about the notorious Cyril Burt whose scientific misdemeanours may well have coloured readers' views about psychometrics such that this chapter will never be properly understood.

Psychometrics was developed, as I said, in Great Britain originally by Spearman at University College London and then by Burt, also an educational psychologist, who set up the first

Educational Psychological Service (in London) and whose main interest was in selecting and evaluating children, especially in respect of their academic potential. Most of Burt's students were or became educational psychologists and gradually psychometrics and factor analysis, the special statistical method developed for the elucidation of tests, became the academic property of Departments of Education rather than psychology. This schism became more pronounced because the only Department of Psychology that was able to compare in prestige and research output with that of University College London under Burt was Cambridge under Bartlett. Bartlett was an experimental psychologist, opposed to statistical analysis, the basis of psychometrics, and as psychology developed in this country professors of psychology trained by Bartlett or influenced by his approach dominated the subject.

This meant that many of the influences that forced experimental psychology to deal with trivia and restrict itself to laboratory experiment did not thus affect psychometrics. Psychometrics indeed concentrated upon real life educational problems and much of its efforts were devoted to what I defined in the first chapter as genuine problems – the determination of intelligence and its nature, and, as Cattell's credo made clear, the study of personality. This has resulted, as I will show, in work that cannot be criticized because it has dealt with trivial problems. Of course, the fact that it has dealt with important issues is no guarantee that it is a good psychology. On the contrary while it may have dealt with them in a superficial way, it nevertheless did so convincingly, such that one could wish that it had left well alone. In this study of psychometrics, therefore, it will not be the triviality of the subject matter *per se* that will have to be explained. Rather I will concentrate upon how the important topics with which it has been concerned have been treated.

Finally before evaluating the work I must deal with the case of Cyril Burt. Burt was responsible for the development of psychometrics in Great Britain, training large numbers of psychometricians and writing influential texts on testing, the statistical methods required in psychometrics, and producing a large flow of empirical results. Two of the most prolific and influential psychometric psychologists, R. B. Cattell and Hans Eysenck, were trained by Burt and to all those in psychometrics it appeared almost heretical when the charge that Burt had faked his twin data appeared. Careful research has shown, almost beyond doubt, that Burt did manufacture these results. However what needs to be said is that this is quite irrelevant to any of the discussions that follow in this chapter. That he faked the data, bearing upon the heritability of intelligence, is irrelevant to the truth or falsity of his claims which must turn on other replicable work. It is quite false to assume that all Burt's views must be wrong or that all psychometrics is similarly dishonest. In this book, however, none of the findings discussed is based upon the work of Burt.

Ability factors

I will first deal with the main results from the psychometric study of human abilities, the original subject matter of psychometrics. One of its achievements, in its own terms, has been to state clearly what are the fundamental dimensions of human ability which can account for the variance and covariance in ability tests and in tasks which would *a priori* appear to demand some ability or abilities to execute them. A small number of broad factors, it is now generally agreed in psychometrics, accounts for much of the variance in tests of ability: fluid ability (general reasoning ability – claimed to be largely genetically determined); crystallized ability, the general ability as it is evinced in the skills valued within a culture; visualization ability, which is involved in all skills where visualization is helpful; retrieval capacity or general fluency, a great aid in creative problem solving, and finally a cognitive speed factor, which shows in speed of writing or computation. A large number of more narrow factors have been found (one of the problems of factor analysis is that potentially the list is endless), of which the most important are: verbal ability, numerical ability, spatial ability, and inductive reasoning.

In the field of human abilities, therefore, it can be said that the main dimensions have been identified. The value of this work, in the practical sphere at least, has been demonstrated over the years in selection. Multiple correlation between these factors and success in jobs ranges from about 0.3 to 0.5, thus enabling selectors for many jobs to do far better than chance allows and than interview or rating methods permit. In the field of educational selection quite good correlations with academic success can be achieved and Vernon has argued that the 11+ selection test for all its problems was remarkably efficient. Too often critics of the ability of psychometric tests to select, forget that it is an actuarial procedure and thus the citation of individual cases which appear clearly to be in error is not entirely relevant. The psychometry of ability has without doubt improved selection and it can be used to improve any selection process.

Previously, I have attempted to show that psychometric tests can be used for vocational guidance. One possibility, which has never been realized, is to build up through research an encyclopaedia of profiles for the successful occupants of various jobs on the main ability (and personality) factors. Then clients could be tested and informed of which jobs suited them most (in terms of resembling their occupants). A similar method involves, rather than profiles, multiple correlations between job success and factor scores. If this were combined with sensitive interviewing, probing the background knowledge of jobs which clients had and their reasons for thinking that they would prefer one occupation to another (although the majority of young people do not know what they want to do), I think vocational guidance would be improved, put onto a more rational basis at least as regards the fit of individual to job.

Thus I would argue that for guidance and selection psychometrics can make a clear and useful contribution. Ability factors have proved the most useful but there can be a genuine gain in predictive power if personality factors (which will be discussed later in this chapter) are included in the research. In sum psychometrics has here provided a valuable, albeit essentially modest, set of tools for selection and guidance.

The factor, or as recent research has shown, the factors of intelligence have been subjected to extensive study in psychometrics and there is now a substantial body of research concerned with the nature of intelligence. One field of intense endeavour has been concerned with the determination of intelligence – to what extent it is heritable or influenced by environmental factors. I shall now try to summarize what has become a complex and highly emotional subject. As I mentioned in the opening chapter, despite the apparent objectivity of intelligence test scores, on this subject there are disparate and quite incompatible views. Thus Kamin, on the one hand, has argued that there is no evidence that would convince a sensible person that intelligence was heritable (1974). On the other extreme some researchers argue that heritability for intelligence, at least in the West, is around 75 per cent. However it has been shown that Kamin's work is flawed and I will put the consensus viewpoint, although I will indicate where there are genuine areas of disagreement. In fact biometric genetic methods overcome many of the problems that lead to these disparate figures and I will briefly describe these before turning to the results themselves.

Biometric methods

Biometric methods were originally designed for agricultural research. Twin studies, which are the simplest approach to the study of heritability, and which are ultimately flawed because it is not possible to correct for the effects of correlated environmental and genetic determinants, are a special case in biometric methods. The essence of biometric genetic analysis is that it breaks down the variance into within and between family variance and is capable of analysing the interaction of genetic and environmental influences. Furthermore, it is able to estimate the fit of various models to the data thus allowing tests for the kind of gene action and mating system in the population. It also allows tests of the complex position when genetic and environmental influences are correlated as may well be the case in human intelligence – intelligent families providing a more stimulating environment than less intelligent families. To achieve all this the data required are the scores on intelligence tests (although any variable can be so analysed) of individuals of every degree of consanguinity – twins, identical and dizygotic, siblings, cousins and so on.

When the biometric methods are used, there is remarkable agreement about the results and it must be stressed that such methods are the basis of the successful, practical programmes in agriculture and horticulture when the production of new varieties is required. In other words these methods work.

There is a considerable genetical component in the determination of the intelligence in European populations. Approximately 70 per cent of the population variance is genetically determined. This means that within a European sample 70 per cent of the variance is attributable to genetic factors. It does not mean that

70 per cent of an individual's intelligence is so determined. It must also be realized that the proportions vary from population to population. Thus in a population where there were huge differences in the environments in which children were raised it would be reasonable to suppose that the proportion of variance attributable to environmental determinants would be greater.

One further point deserves mention. It should not be thought that this relatively high genetic determination of intelligence means that intelligence test scores are immutable. On the contrary it can be shown that with an 80 per cent heritability (a figure higher than the highest estimate) environmentally determined changes even as large as 20–30 percentage points could be possible, on a standard intelligence test – a very large difference.

There are several points that I want to make about these findings from the biometric analysis of intelligence, and they illustrate, again, the problems with the scientific study of psychology even in one of its more successful fields. First, it is ironical to note that the results are highly similar to the false findings of Burt. There is no doubt that had he bothered to collect and analyse his data, he would have been able to confirm the views that he passionately held. Furthermore, the findings demonstrate beyond all equivocation that intelligence tests (measuring both fluid and crystallized intelligence) cannot simply measure ability at intelligence tests, as some critics have argued. It is simply not conceivable that ability at a particular set of items, unrelated to anything else in the world, could be at all genetically determined. High heritability indices confirm that the test scores have an underlying physiological basis and hence are related to other variables with a similar basis. Of course, that intelligence test scores do measure something more than skill at intelligence tests is also confirmed by correlations with academic and job success which are always positive and sometimes considerable in size.

In the chapter which dealt with models of memory, one of the most stringent criticisms uses not their inexactitude but their inutility. It was not clear what could be done with the knowledge either practically or theoretically. A detailed description of, say, recall was thus unlike the detailed description of an organism, for example. Consequently the question must be answered: what is the value, in any way, of this knowledge that approximately 70 per cent of the population variance in Great Britain is determined genetically?

In my view the utility of this work is small. What has been shown is that both the environment and an individual's genetic endowment contribute to his or her intelligence. However what effect does this have on, say, teaching or hiring a person for a job? All that matters is how a person performs. It is true that if we see a child from an obviously disadvantaged background performing badly we could hope to see an improvement if the educational opportunities available were improved. However this would still be the case if the proportions were reversed. Indeed let us assume the two most extreme cases, to see what value this biogenetic knowledge might have. If it had been shown that intelligence was entirely genetic, quite unaltered by anything that happened to an individual (an absurd proposition quite alien to experience), this would not mean that we would give up trying to educate people of low intelligence. The fact is education is about far more than the development of intelligence. Again if it were shown to be entirely environmentally determined this would have little practical effect. In other words the establishment of the proportions of population variance in intelligence test scores is of no practical value whatever. If such psychological biometrics are a useful exercise, the utility must be theoretical.

As I mentioned previously, biometric genetic methods were devised in agricultural and horticultural research. Here with more genetically simple characteristics such as resistance to cold weather, rich fruiting, flavour and freedom from disease, the methods had practical and commercial application – the production of varieties with desired characteristics. These methods have been shown to be correct because the requisite varieties and breeds have been produced.

Thus the equivalent practical application in the case of intelligence would be the breeding of a master race of superbly intelligent individuals. I do not intend to discuss this aspect further other than to say that, with multigenetic characteristics such as intelligence, such a breeding programme would be impossible in practice. Ethically, also, such a programme is offensive in the extreme. Thus, that its practical value is nugatory is not a reflection on biometric genetics but rather a reflection on its application to the field of intelligence.

From a theoretical viewpoint the results are not meaningless but are somewhat banal. Thus if it had been shown that intelligence was entirely genetically determined, our ideas on the impact of experience would have had to be dramatically changed. Similarly in the total environmental instance we would have to suppose that our neural apparatus had no effect on our ability to reason, both inferences that deny experience and make nonsense of all our current notions of what goes to constitute the sum total of a human being. As it is, the finding that there are both genetic and environmental determinants of intelligence is not surprising. What is important here, theoretically, is what are these environmental determinants and how do they inhibit or increase intelligence?

In summary, I am again forced into the position that, despite the sophistication and power of biometric analysis of intelligence, there is actually little of either theoretical or practical value that has emerged. Perhaps its only use is to form a corrective to the extreme political dogmas of the left and right. Here at least is evidence that both camps, stressing the environmental or the genetic position, are wrong, but, really, most individuals commonsensically take up the middle ground without recourse to the mathematical complexities of biometrics.

Racial differences in intelligence

I will now deal briefly with a related topic which unquestionably is one in which non-psychologists are interested (here there is no disjunction between psychometric and popular interest). This concerns racial differences in intelligence. First a misconception must be removed. Even if it is accepted that *within* any one cultural group there is a considerable genetic component determining intellectual ability, then it is *not* legitimate to argue that differences in intelligence between races are genetically determined. There is no logical step to bridge the gap of within group and between group differences.

A second and quite separate point concerns the origins of the differences to be found among racial groups when examining their intelligence test scores. Much work comparing American Blacks with other American groups indicates that Blacks score about fifteen points lower on average, even when variables such as social class and parental education are controlled. Jensen has argued that these differences are genetically determined simply because other environmental determinants, such as bias in the test items, different attitudes to testing, different motivation, suspicion of the White establishment, just for example, can be shown to be insufficient to produce the findings, although this interpretation has been challenged.

Beyond the United States context there is further work attempting to compare the intelligence of different racial or cultural groups. Claims have been made that the most intelligent are the Mongoloids, Japanese, and Chinese, closely followed by Jews who are certainly a culturally defined rather than a racial group. At the bottom of this intellectual pecking order again come the Black Africans. Anthropologists and cross-cultural psychologists have again challenged these findings, criticizing the application of the same test in different cultures on the grounds that items are simply not equivalent in meaning even if the item statistics are similar. They further argue that meaning and salience of intelligence varies so strongly across cultures that meaningful cross-cultural comparison is impossible.

What is the practical and theoretical value of comparing the intelligence of different cultural and racial groups? As far as practical application goes, there is none that I can think of. It must be remembered that even when comparing the highest with the lowest group there is a considerable overlap of distributions such that knowing an individual's race gives you little chance of predicting his intelligence. On account of the above, there is little of practical value. Furthermore, as was the case with the work on heritability, grave ethical problems would arise if we were to try to select individuals for intelligence on the basis of race. Consequently the practical value of this work is nil.

Theoretically the cross-cultural comparison of groups is of a little more interest, provided that (and this is a large proviso that as yet cannot be met) the tests allow fair comparison. If for a moment we grant that the technical cross-cultural testing problems are overcome, it might be possible to discern the cultural influences on the test scores, thus leading to an understanding of some of the environmental, experiential determinants of intelligence. While this is perhaps a possibility, other cultural differences such as attitudes to testing and tests, the emphasis on speed and accuracy in a culture, test familiarity, the difficulty of developing equivalent items across cultures and the salience of intelligence in cultures are difficult to disentangle from the theoretically interesting cultural determinants. Consequently I am forced to conclude that, while there could be a theoretical pay-off from the cross-cultural study of intelligence in respect of its environmental determinants, this is as yet not realizable and may never reliably be so. Its practical application is certainly nil.

Personality factors

I shall now leave the psychometrics of ability and turn instead to the psychometrics of personality. This field is now half a century old and has been pursued by some of the finest psychometrists. Once again I shall set out the main findings and then scrutinize their practical and theoretical utility.

The psychometric study of personality was greatly influenced by and followed closely the pattern of the work on human abilities. This meant that one of the strategies most used was to search by factor analysis for the major dimensions of personality. However, whereas for abilities there is agreement among the results of different investigators, this is far from the case regarding personality. Indeed it is almost literally true to say that there are as many sets of factors as there are factor analytic researchers. However recently, with the help of my colleague Paul Barrett, now at the Institute of Psychiatry with Eysenck, I have searched the factor analytic results having regard to proper methodology and interpretation of results. We concluded that four basic dimensions of personality had emerged from fifty years of research. These are: (1) extraversion (sociability, openness, outward looking) with introversion (inward looking, aloof, inhibited) at the other pole; (2) neuroticism (the tendency to worry and be anxious, a trait which should not be confused with the state of anxiety, being anxious at or before some discrete event); (3) psychoticism (toughmindedness, sensation seeking, cruelty); and (4) obsessionality (including neatness, control, pedantry, rigidity which results in some cultures in the authoritarian personality – characterized by the petty official in a superlatively ironed, immaculate uniform, hair and moustache under perfect control, obeying regulations to the letter, ruthlessly harsh to those below him, and sycophantically obedient, cringing to his superiors, the building block of totalitarianism).

As was the case with the factorial study of abilities, these factors have shown themselves useful in selecting for jobs and in initial screening procedures for stressful tasks such as are necessary in the armed services or the police. For example, extroverts are good at jobs requiring personal interaction; introverts are well suited to posts which entail being on one's own for long periods. In a recent study which I have made of the effects of sleeplessness on human abilities, it was discovered that in a really tough sergeants' training course the drop-outs could be predicted from their scores involving the neuroticism factor.

In the fields of clinical psychology and psychosomatic medicine, both neuroticism and psychoticism are important psychological variables. To draw again on some of the research with my students, I found that neuroticism was related to recovery in heart patients after the insertion of pacemakers and played a role in frequent attendance at the general practitioner. Thus at the practical level of selection and screening the psychometric study of personality has produced a small number of useful variables.

At the theoretical level both Cattell and Eysenck have attempted to develop theories of personality using the basic factors as the main variables. However, the complexity of human personality is such that these efforts, heroic and ingenious though they be, cannot be described as wholly successful. Nevertheless, the claim that any good personality theory should at least include these variables within it, rather than rely exclusively on them, is not unreasonable. At the level of theory, therefore, this aspect of the psychometric contribution is limited but is, nevertheless, not entirely negligible. Important variables have been discovered.

In summary I maintain that the psychometric search for the basic dimensions of personality has proved useful for occupational selection and clinical screening, a modest but worthwhile contribution to applied psychology. At the theoretical level this work is also valuable but is too limited to base a grand theory upon.

Before leaving this factor analytic work on personality, there is a more general point that needs to be made. Factor analysis, as it is used in psychometrics, seeks to establish the underlying dimensions that can mathematically account for the correlations between variables. It is, therefore, concerned with individual differences on the common dimensions which people share. In the field of abilities this seems no disadvantage since it makes good sense to think of problem solving in terms of major abilities such as verbal ability, numerical ability and general intelligence. These would appear to embrace a large variety of different skills. In the field of personality, however, while it is still meaningful to conceptualize it in terms of a number of common variables, there is another universe of variables or influences, those based upon the individual, personal experiences of life – the subject matter, of course, of psychoanalysis and all human psychology. These experiences seem to most people the most important and meaningful of their lives: how they get on with their parents and siblings, their friends and lovers, their experiences at school and work, for example, of birth and death, of joy and sadness. Not even identical twins share this essence of living which is different for every person, and upon these individual experiences factor analysis cannot impinge from its statistical nature.

Furthermore, although I fully agree that quantification is the soul of science and that the factor analytic variables which I have described are measured as precisely as possible, I cannot believe that the richness of human personality as we see it around us is caught by scores on extraversion, neuroticism, psychoticism and obsessionality, in whatever combination. Is it really possible that Buddha, Jesus Christ, Bach, Shakespeare, Da Vinci, Newton, Freud, Hitler, Ghandi, Myra Hindley and I differ just in our combinations on these variables? To one who answers that question positively, I reply that there are more things in heaven and earth than are dreamed of in your philosophy. That is why I described the contributions of factor analysis to personality as useful but limited, especially theoretically.

Factor analysis and educational psychology: an example

There is an extension of psychometrics, which I shall now discuss, in which psychometric methods are brought to bear upon important problems. I shall illustrate the method by a study of primary school education conducted in the early 1960s in the University of Manchester School of Education. This was a fine example of how certain problems are amenable to psychometric analysis. The department was asked by the Government to determine the bases of educational achievement at primary school. To answer this question a large sample of children was given a battery of attainment and ability tests and in addition measures of their environment and schools were obtained, for example, class sizes, teacher qualifications, education and social class of parents, number of books in the household, attitudes of parents to schools. The whole matrix of variables was then subjected to factor analysis. The rationale of this approach was simple: all those variables which loaded on the same factor as educational achievement were *ipso facto* associated with achievement (note *not* necessarily the determinants of it). In fact the results were surprising in that school variables played little part. The most important of all was the mother's attitude as measured by the variable 'lice in hair'.

To factor analyse a huge matrix of variables in this way provides a neat answer to the problem and I think where relatively restricted questions, with clear criteria such as educational success, are asked, this general psychometric approach can be effective. Recently Penny Pickering working with me has used the same technique to investigate the patients of a general practice who take tranquillizers (1986). Here again it proved valuable in uncovering some of the factors which are associated with such attendance. However it has to be noted that a more clinical, less quantified approach was necessary to uncover the subtleties of this behaviour. The psychometric approach identified fairly gross variables, for example no friends or broken marriages. In brief this extension of the method is useful for clear, precise questions especially where a large number of variables is involved. However after these gross findings, more fine grained analysis is required and for this psychometrics is not well attuned. This was true for our educational illustration. Thus the measures of attitude and school atmosphere were crude as were the attainment tests, if it is considered that schools do more than teach some basic content. For a real understanding of these matters a far more clinical approach would be necessary. Nevertheless for making a preliminary assay through complex material, this psychometric, factor analytic approach can be useful.

The study of love

As a final illustration of these limitations, I want to scrutinize a study of love by Sternberg at Yale University. This is a particularly useful example for my thesis because it tackles a subject which even the most ardent behaviourist would have to admit was important (unfortunate though it be) and significant in the lives of almost everybody, a mere epiphenomenon. Furthermore, Sternberg is one of the leading psychometrists in the world with a large number of excellent and original books in the field of intelligence. Thus I am about to scrutinize just about the best quality work that could be done on a subject which is not irrelevant to real human concerns. If this is successful then psychometrics in good hands, can be said to be valuable. If it fails, however, it foretells doom other than in simple applied research.

Sternberg's paper is concerned with the nature of love (1984). It is, therefore, involved with one of the central topics of human psychology. Unquestionably this is a study that goes to the heart of the matter. One of the aims of the research, and perhaps the main aim, was to compare three alternative structural models of the nature of love. In addition the validity of these models was examined, and the predictive power for the success of close relationships from some of the love scales used in the study was put to the test.

The first point to comment upon is the singularity of the aim. A structural model may well be useful in many scientific or psychological topics but it is by no means obvious that a structural model of love is even a sensible way of conceptualizing the subject. This misgiving is supported by the fact that the study sought to compare three models – a Spearman unifactorial entity, unitary and one that cannot be decomposed; a Thomsonian model, comprising a large number of affective, cognitive and motivational bonds which are sampled when we experience love; and a Thurstonian entity which comprises a small number of primary factors, correlated and equally salient in the experience of love. My misgivings that it may be misconceived even to attempt to develop a model of love are strengthened by these particular models which are taken over from the psychometric study of intelligence. Thus the first and original factor analytic model of intelligence was the concept of intelligence as g, a unitary reasoning ability – Spearman's brilliant contribution to psychology which, albeit in a revised form, has stood the test of time. This was challenged by Godfrey Thomson in Edinburgh, whose sampling model of intelligence accounted for the fact that there seemed to be a general ability factor and other primary abilities. Elements consisted of branching of brain cells, synaptic conductivity, production of neurochemical transmitters, for example. If cognitive tasks utilized many of these elements in common, they would be correlated highly. If only a few were common, the correlations would be small. Cognitive tests, therefore, load on the g factor according to the number of such elements which are involved in their solution. Thurstone's model claimed that cognitive performance depended upon a number of primary mental abilities, for example verbal or spatial ability. These, however, were correlated, correlations that could be accounted for by the general factor of intelligence.

These three models of intelligence were developed to account for the findings of the factor analysis of human abilities, when it became clear that a single factor plus a specific test factor were not a sufficient account of the structure of abilities. In this paper Sternberg seeks to test which of the three models best accounts for the structure of love, as measured by some love scales (which I shall examine later in this section). However, no rationale for deciding to compare these three models is given, and Sternberg writes that no one had attempted to do such a thing before.

Thus the question arises as to why these three models of the structure of love were chosen. I shall assume perhaps charitably that they were not chosen at random, charitably because experimental psychologists love to select things using randomized blocks or random number tables – the scientist's I Ching. The only rational assumption to explain the choice, since none was given, is that Sternberg has reason to believe that the structure of love resembles the structure of intelligence. However I can see no obvious reason why this should be so. Indeed I can see, a priori, every reason why it should not be so. Problem solving appears to involve certain reasoning processes operating in various media – spatial, verbal and so on. Love, which is notoriously difficult to define or pin down, would not appear remotely similar with its confusion of feelings and emotions, memories and hopes. There seems no more reason to choose models developed from the study of human abilities than to choose models from any other sphere at all. Why not atomic particle models which resemble love in their polarity of attraction and rejection and in their immense potential energy? Of course, to choose models to test limits and define the research. Without a clear theoretical rationale this is a dubious method. Far better it would seem to find a model, of any kind, that would fit the data and then replicate it on a different sample.

There is one other possibility to account for this experimental design. If this be its *raison d'être*, it is a serious commentary upon scientific methods. The structure of human abilities was elucidated by factor analysing ability tests. The structure of human personality was elucidated by factor analysing personality tests. Perhaps, therefore, factoring love scales will elucidate the structure of love. Now the factor analysis of abilities has been relatively successful. This is partly due to the fact that good ability tests are fairly easy to construct, because the test items can sample the actual ability. Thus a mathematical ability item is mathematics and requires mathematical ability to solve it, as is the case with other abilities. The factor analysis of personality has achieved less because personality tests are far more difficult to construct than are tests of ability. This is because the items are not samples of what we want to measure but, often, self-reports from which inferences about personality are made. In the case of love, therefore, much must depend on whether or not the love scales used can really measure love or not. The nature of the love scales must, therefore, be carefully scrutinized. Clearly much will turn on the validity of the love scales.

Five scales of liking and loving were used. The first was a series of bipolar adjectives. Subjects had to note their ideal romantic love relationship on seven point scales for each of these twenty adjectives. Examples of these were: long-short, slow-fast, hot-cold, logical-intuitive, systematic-unsystematic. The second scale was a 'limerence' scale, 'limerence' referring to the feeling of being in love. There are in this scale sixty-six items describing love of which a typical example is 'I love everything about someone to whom I am strongly attached' or 'I have felt an intense attraction for someone I hardly know'. The third scale was a fifty-item scale with six sub-scales: logical love, unselfish love, game-playing love, romantic love, possessive love, best friend love. The fourth instrument has fifty-seven items, questions and ratings, for example, 'How easily can X gain the admiration of others?' or 'How concerned are you about X's welfare?' Subjects completed this Rubin scale, as it referred to their relationship with their mother, father, sibling who was nearest in age, oldest child, best same-sex friend and present or most recent lover or spouse. The fifth and last of these scales of loving and liking was a forty-one item scale consisting of phrases describing aspects of love such as 'offering emotional support to other'. Subjects rated the same six relationships as above on seven-point scales. These and other scales of personality and demographic background were given to thirty-five men and fifty women of whom fifty-seven were single, sixteen married, the rest in various combinations of tortured matrimony.

The main aim of the work centred on the factor analysis of the two most important love scales, the fourth and fifth scales, the Rubin and the Levinger scales. From both of these a highly similar first factor emerged accounting for about half the variance in the data. The other factors in the scales were small and clearly of little importance. Thus Sternberg argued that the Thurstonian model had to be rejected (for a number of primary factors would have been expected) and that the results supported either a Spearman or Thomson model, which are both unifactorial. However an hierarchical cluster analysis of the factors showed that the items formed clusters, thus supporting Thomson rather than Spearman. It was concluded that a Thomsonian sampling model of love accounts best for its nature.

In this study all hinges on the scales. Scale number four measuring love had items with the following meanings: I enjoy giving X a present, I would be willing to do many things for X, I am much concerned about X's welfare, I love X very much, I am happy with X, I would feel bad if I couldn't be with X. The highest loading item was the first: I enjoy giving X a present. Scale four had items loading on the factor: I have interests the other shares, I share ideas and information, we grow personally through the relationship, we discover new interests together, we understand the other well, we make the other feel needed. The evidence that these were truly measures of love was supported by the fact that there were positive correlations between these scales and success in their love relationship.

There are many comments that could be made about this research which follows the classic psychometric approach to the study of love, as was used in the original research into intelligence. Do these scales measure love? The fact that they can predict the success of a relationship is hardly surprising. If one is concerned with another's welfare and likes to be with him or her, and likes to share information (to cite a few items), it is likely that the relationship will be better than with an individual who was unconcerned with the other's welfare, hated to be with the other and never shared information. It takes a factor analysis to reveal that, no doubt. This does not mean the scales measure love.

Readers, think back on your own experiences of love. Does this litany of items capture the elation, the happiness, the despair? Is love described by these items loadings on the factors?

Scale 5

Item	Loading
Having interests the other shares	0.83
Sharing ideas and information	0.82
Growing personally through the relationship	0.80
Discovering new interests together	0.79
Understanding the other well	0.79
Making the other feel needed	0.78
Receiving help from the other	0.77
Helping the other to grow personally	0.76
Sharing deeply personal ideas and feelings	0.75
Having no secrets from each other	0.74
Receiving affection from the other	0.70
Receiving emotional support from the other	0.68
Needing the other person	0.66
Listening to the other's confidences	0.64
Giving help to the other	0.61
Offering emotional support to the other	0.61
Giving affection to the other	0.60

Scale 4

Item	Loading
How much would you enjoy giving X a present?	0.85
How many things would you be willing to do for X?	0.84
How concerned are you about X's welfare?	0.83

How much would you say that you love X?	0.82
In general, how happy do you feel when you are with X?	0.73
How bad would you feel if you could never be with X?	0.72
To what extent do you think your and X's personalities complement each other?	0.71
How much confidence do you have in X's good judgement?	0.67
How easily can X gain respect from others?	0.64
How many common interests do you and X have?	0.64

(These are the best loading items in the paper by Sternberg.)
Or does some of the finest poetry of Shakespeare describe love?

> Love's not time's fool, though rosy lips and cheeks
> Within his bending Sickle's compass come:
> Love alters not with his brief hours and weeks
> But bears it out even to the edge of doom.
> If this be error and upon me proved
> I never writ nor no man ever loved.

What these scales are measuring is not love but statements about love, cognitions rather than emotions. The internal structure of love, as it is experienced, cannot be recovered from this list of banalities.

Actually even on a less important level Sternberg's study is seriously flawed. I fail to see how generalizations about the structure of love can be made from the structure of two scales, even if it were accepted that they were valid. The hundred or so items are only a tiny subset of the whole universe of love items. Furthermore the fact that hierarchical cluster analysis broke the general factor up is more a function of the cluster analysis than the structure of the construct which the items are supposed to measure. In any case even if there are clusters of items they must be highly correlated or else they would not load the general factor. There is no end to analyses one could make and the split between primary and secondary factors is ultimately arbitrary. Finally, even if the clusters were accepted as valid, they in no way resemble a Thomsonian model which referred to neurological biochemical elements. The elements in this model, cognition, emotions, affects, are simply items of the original scale. The analogy with Thomson's intelligence model is superficial in the extreme.

If this be the scientific contribution to the study of love, long may science and love remain divorced. Surely it requires that intelligent psychologists suspend their disbelief when they carry out this research almost as if this study were a work of theatre. Alas it is not a farce or joke, nor a black comedy; but it is a tragedy. Surely it supports the title of this chapter – that psychometrics renders the soul to ashes and confirms the claim that scientific psychology is an attempt to deny emotion. Love has long defied definition by poets and philosophers so let us define it to end this analysis by its highest loading item: 'I would very much enjoy giving – a present.'

Conclusions

In brief, from this chapter I think the following conclusions stand out. Unlike other branches of psychology, for social and institutional reasons, psychometrics has not devoted itself to trivial questions, although inevitably much of psychometrics is concerned with relatively unimportant technical problems. On the contrary it has tackled large issues and ones of great practical importance. In applied psychology, especially in selection and to a less extent in guidance, psychometrics can make a genuine and useful contribution. A well constructed and validated psychometric test is a more efficient measure than a clinical interview. However this kind of applied psychology, although valuable, is simple. Psychometrics can make a more general and more theoretically important contribution when the methods are used to explore complex problems such as the determinants of educational achievement or the use of tranquillizers as I have described, even though the results need skilful amplification through other methods. However, more subtle topics are limited by the crude and inferential nature of even the best psychometric tests. As I have shown, even when carried out by one of the most thoughtful psychometrists, such topics, exemplified by love, are rendered inane. Thus psychometrics can answer some concrete applied questions but beyond this it is defeated.

Chapter five

Attitudes, attributions, and group processes in the laboratory and beyond

In this chapter I shall discuss and examine some of the main findings from social psychology concerning attitudes and group processes. Social psychology, like the psychometrics discussed in the previous chapter, ostensibly deals with topics that most people consider to be important, hence, again, I shall be concerned with investigating to what extent this ostensible link to the real world is itself real. This question is particularly important because social psychology has developed away from orthodox experimental psychology so that it could devote itself to the 'scientific study of human social behaviour', the feeling being that experimental psychology had strayed too far from human concerns.

Laboratory games

First I shall scrutinize the research carried out on group processes and interactions, which have been studied in social psychology by the invention of various laboratory games that allow such processses and strategies of co-operation and competition to be observed along with the conditions that give rise to them. These experimental games, as Professor Eiser, my colleague in Exeter, has pointed out, were social psychology's equivalent of the laboratory experiment in experimental psychology. There seems little doubt that a large element in making such games popular was the ease with which experimental conditions could be manipulated and quantified results obtained, thus resulting in a body of research work, much as was the case with the models of memory discussed in Chapter 3. In addition the rationale of these games – a sensible pay-off matrix could be developed by the players –

was that man was rational, and they were, in their time, a counter-blast to psychoanalytically oriented approaches to social behaviour which, naturally, stressed the unconscious determinants of such behaviour.

I shall not describe all the games which social psychologists have used in their attempts to elucidate the nature of human interaction but I shall concentrate upon the one which has been extensively researched.

The Prisoner's Dilemma game

This is an imaginary situation in which two prisoners are about to be tried. If neither informs, each will receive moderate sentences; if one informs, he receives a light sentence but the other receives a severe sentence; while if both inform both receive moderately severe sentences and thus would be worse off than if they had not done so. Each has to make up his mind independently and the dilemma, obviously, turns around whether each can trust the other not to inform.

Translated into experimental form, there are a series of trials in which each of the two participants can make either a co-operative or a defective response. The outcome for each trial (a monetary reward) depends on the response of each of the players. Eiser in his book *Cognitive Social Psychology* has a neat pay-off matrix showing what the rewards will be for each player, depending on the responses.

Obviously the relative size of the rewards affects the player's decisions as to whether they co-operate or not. Thus A will always do better if he chooses D regardless of what B does. However, the reward is small if B uses this strategy as well. Jointly, each will better be to choose C, but if one defects, the other pays heavily for it – hence the dilemma.

I do not intend to discuss any of the results obtained from the Prisoner's Dilemma, because its relevance to my thesis is independent of any results. The point at issue is simply whether or not this game resembles any situation in the real world such that it is reasonable to extrapolate the results to anything else at all, other than similar games.

Eiser, who is a social psychologist, makes a number of comments upon it that deserve attention. First, he admits that the

Figure 5.1 Pay-off matrix for the Prisoner's Dilemma game

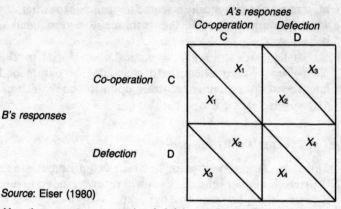

Source: Eiser (1980)

where X = the monetary rewards of A (above diagonal) and B (below diagonal) and:

$$X_3 > X_1 > X_4 > X_2;$$
$$2X_1 > (X_2 + X_3) > 2X_4.$$

These prizes or rewards, it will be seen, exactly reflect the original description of the Prisoner's Dilemma.

Prisoner's Dilemma is an artificial situation on account of the fact that responses are so limited and that there is no communication between players. In addition players have to move before each knows the other's decision. If this were not the case, of course, there would be no dilemma. The pay-off matrix allows one to make the best choice in the light of any response. Similarly if the relative values of the rewards for the different classes were different, then so too would be the results. Eiser therefore admits that the game does not resemble most situations beyond the laboratory. All these criticisms are serious and I am fully in agreement with them. Indeed I would argue that these points alone render the findings from the Prisoner's Dilemma of little value for understanding social interactions in the real world, except, perhaps, in those rare cases where the situation does resemble the game. However, even here, if any such cases there be, I would argue that nothing could be deduced from the Prisoner's Dilemma because of an even more serious and fundamental flaw, which Eiser does not raise.

Before I discuss this: however, I want to scrutinize Eiser's counter-argument to the criticisms raised in the previous paragraph which I regard as rendering the game worthless. Eiser's counter is this: an understanding of social behaviour arises from an understanding of the interaction between any given social structure and the cognitive processes of the individuals involved and this can be studied as well in one situation as any other. Such, then, is Eiser's rebuttal of these points.

Ingenious as this argument is, alas it will not do. It assumes that the interaction between process and structure is the same, regardless of structure. But what evidence is there that this is the case? If it is not the same, clearly it is necessary to study the interaction in structures that actually exist. If it is the same, why is it that variables such as communication or no communication affect findings? All that can be seen from the Prisoner's Dilemma is that there is an interaction. Since it is an artificial situation, unlike most in the real world, extrapolation is difficult.

Eiser's assumption of communality turns on the notion of game: 'what is important is how they define the game'. This, then, is the useful information that comes from the Prisoner's Dilemma, and Eiser claims that roles and games are played outside the laboratory, that interaction itself is a game. This may well be so, but it so extends the meaning of 'game' as to render the term valueless. If everything can be defined as a game what does the term signify? Furthermore, despite the claims that understanding the interaction of process and structure within the Prisoner's Dilemma is what is of value, no such conclusions are drawn by Eiser from his survey of his work. I still feel that Eiser's argument does not stand scrutiny. The original criticisms, that extrapolation from such artificial games to real-life is dubious, still hold.

However, there is far more serious criticism of the Prisoner's Dilemma, and indeed all laboratory games, that seems to me to render the whole gamut of such games scientifically valueless. Unless it is shown, and this has not been done, that there is an external validity to the findings from these games, then the a priori criticism, that the game itself is so pointless that there is no reason to think subjects are engaged in it in any real way, is devastating. If one were a prisoner, the dilemma for both parties would be absolutely critical. To sit in a psychological laboratory and indicate which of two choices one makes having regard to a pay-off matrix is so tedious that I am surprised that responses are more than random. The variables that affect performance in the game can never be extrapolated to real life where social situations have some meaning for the participants. It is this denial of the meaning of social situations, their emotional force, that allows psychologists even to conceive of using a game such as the Prisoner's Dilemma. As in the case of experimental psychology, research in the Prisoner's Dilemma is founded upon repression of feeling and emotion, and upon the denial of meaning. This objection, the lack of emotional significance of the Prisoner's Dilemma for the players, compared with a real-life social situation, even a boring one such as a committee meeting, applies to all such games. It could be objected by a defender of these methods, that meaning can be manipulated experimentally in the laboratory. I fear that this is yet another fantasy of the experimenter. Even the well-known experiments of Milgram (1974), who persuaded people ostensibly to give electric shocks to subjects by a deceptive experimental procedure which once known can never be again administered, are not wholly convincing. It is almost impossible that a scientific experimenter would put a subject at serious risk. One of the fundamental beliefs of educational institutions in the West is the probably mistaken one that they operate for the good of mankind. That is the essence of education even if 'mankind' is defined narrowly, as it was in Nazi Germany. Educational institutions are not allowed to kill people and take precautions that they do not do so. Thus Milgram's subjects at some level were not probably taken in. In any case to give shocks in those conditions is not as horrific as the killing of civilians in military duty – which is actually contrary to military law. Even if Milgram could set up a convincing experiment, how anybody could convince a subject that the Prisoner's Dilemma had any significance is quite another story.

Eiser admits that extrapolations from one game to a different game are difficult enough so that, given all the problems I have discussed, the question arises as to why there is so substantial a body of research on these games. The clue lies in the repression and denial of feeling and meaning. Such repression is unconscious and it results in no feeling being perceived. Thus there is nothing lacking, in these experiments, to those who deny feelings. Furthermore, as was the case with memory models, given the Prisoner's Dilemma, a well-trained social psychologist can easily produce papers deemed publishable by his peers. By so producing papers a considerable knowledge of variables and factors affecting the Prisoner's Dilemma and other similar games has been built up. This is almost pure hermeneutics, the study of tasks invented and elaborated by those who study them. As I have now made clear I cannot see how a study of such games, however they resemble in some respects the real world, can ever lead to anything but a knowledge of such games.

Attribution theory

I now want to turn to an aspect of social psychology that is of increasing importance. Indeed it has begun to affect thinking about human personality and has led psychologists to challenge notions of traits and patterns of personality. This whole field is attribution theory.

One of the minor achievements of psychometrics, I argued in Chapter 4, was its establishment of a small number of personality traits based upon the factor analysis of personality questionnaires. These traits, extraversion and neuroticism, are the two largest in terms of the variance which they account for, and not only have a statistical basis but have been shown to correlate with a variety of external criteria and to have substantive heritability indices.

Attribution theory, on the contrary, regards personality traits not so much as characteristics of individuals but rather as notions in the mind's eye of the observer. Thus in attribution theory, extraversion is not a trait at all, but is a construct which an observer uses to account for his observations of an individual. Extraversion, as is the case with all traits, cannot be observed. It is an inference based upon seeing an individual, say, talking loudly, being cheerful and refusing to contemplate his problems. Thus we explain the behaviour by saying that X does these things because he is extraverted. Actually attribution theory goes beyond this in that it is claimed that individuals attempt to understand their entire social milieu in terms of attributions. People, it is claimed in this wider theory, first put forward by Heider, attribute causes to social events, impersonal, external to the person, and internal, such as ability and personality variables. Personal attributions imply that the individual intended the particular outcome, and if it is clear that the observed behaviour was controlled by an external event, no personal attributions are made. For example if, in a church service, the vicar rises to give a sermon no personal attributions are made from this event about his volubility or his narcissism, nor is any such imputation made from the peculiar ecclesiastical undulance of the voice. However, if such a voice were heard beyond the church, and not from a vicar, some curious attributions would be made. Where external events cannot be seen to determine behaviour, we attribute internal causes – such as traits.

As Eiser has argued there are problems with this attributional theory. The worst of these concerns the place and nature of intention. This is because to make an attribution of, say, a personality trait, the observer has to attribute intention to the actor, since, obviously, if the outcome of an act were unintended, we could not make attributions about the causes of this act. However, although this is entailed by the theory it is certainly not so. For example, if a person slams a glass down hard on the table, and does not look surprised and horrified when he breaks it, the outcome was, presumably, intended. An attributional theorist might then infer that he was a violent and uncontrolled person, especially if he gave no sign of being annoyed. This exemplifies, in theory, how the attribution of intention preceded the attribution of traits. However if the individual did look surprised and horrified when it broke, we would presume it was unintentional. However that does not mean that we make no attributions. On the contrary, we can attribute clumsiness and even stupidity to the person who does this. Thus even on intuitive grounds the link between intentionality and attribution is not as simple as the theory maintains.

However there are even more severe problems with the very notion of intentionality. It is possible to intend to do something with a particular set of consequences in mind, when in fact a totally different set of consequences may come about as a result of taking action. For example, I may intend to drive to work in order to write this book. However if I have an accident the consequences of my driving may result in death or injury, and certainly no book will be written, that day at least. Or again, as I write my book, I may strain my hand and eyesight and hurt my back since I am in fact writing in a very poor posture. Indeed it is possible to fail in one's intentions. I may cook the dinner in order to appease my wife and the dinner may be good and eaten yet there may be no appeasement. In fact the action may have the opposite effect: if you can do it now, why not before?

There is a further problem with the notion of intent which is not discussed by Eiser but which is also important in evaluating attribution theory and which, in my view, exemplifies its weakness. If we adopt a psychodynamic position the notion of intention becomes exceedingly weak. It seems to me that there is ample evidence in the case studies of psychoanalysis that we do things for unconscious reasons. In other words there are more than the two classes of determinants – external or internal (intentional) – which are used in attribution theory. For example, as in the case of slips and errors, at least in some instances the putative error was intended by the person, although this intention was below the level of awareness and was thus not conscious. If I wash up and smash a good deal of crockery, the unconscious intention was, on this model, to destroy the crockery, in order to get my own back, although whether it is sensible to call such a desire intentional is another matter and not relevant to this argument. Thus from a number of viewpoints this attribution theory of personality is clearly unsatisfactory.

However there are further points which need to be made before the theory can be properly evaluated. The first is a simple logical point. Suppose an observer notes that an individual, for no obvious external reason, seems ill at ease, is sweating, clutches his stomach, takes some magnesia, keeps looking at the clock, and adjusting his clothes and generally has a somewhat lean and hungry look, as he strides about the room like a caged tiger. He just might conclude, provided he was not an experimental psychologist, that this individual was anxious, that is, high on the trait of anxiety. This is the attribution accounting for the behaviour.

Suppose, however, as was claimed in Chapter 4 and as is strongly held by Eysenck, that there is a trait of anxiety largely dependent on the lability of the autonomic nervous system, and that this individual is high on this variable. That our observer infers that he is neurotic is a function of what? Of his attributions or the fact that the subject is high on the trait? Of course every statement is a reflection of the person who makes it but because this applies to everything, to point it out says nothing. In other words attribution theory is only meaningful if there are no traits, or any other characteristics. If there are, it means little more than that observers can make inferences from what they observe. So attributional theories of personality are not about personality but how people make judgements about personality, not a topic of great import on the criteria adopted in this book. Why personality rather than any other topic?

This effectively is the second point. Take away the jargon and the formal statements of the theory and attribution theory describes, as was argued above, the way in which people judge the personality of others. Essentially it claims that where no external influence can be seen, observers infer there are internal influences. This does not appear to be a powerfully imaginative theory. It would be difficult to see how it could be otherwise.

Studies of how people make these judgements of personality are, in effect, studies of their implicit theories of personality unless it is assumed that there are real characteristics which give rise to the attributions. But if this latter is assumed, attributions are uninteresting unless it is argued that regular distortions of these characteristics take place. This, however, has not been claimed. While a person's implicit theories of personality are clearly a viable subject of study, this is a far cry from studying actual personality itself. Indeed there is an absurd paradox in attribution theory. There is no such entity as personality, it is all attributable to people's theories about personality, which by definition must be wrong, unless – and this again is the case – subjects realize that all is attribution. However, if all is attribution there must be a basis for it and we are into an infinite regress.

In brief, attribution theory is really a simplistic claim that people make judgements about personality arising from their implicit theories which seem, in perfect sense, to claim that external and internal forces contribute to behaviour. This is a banal theory which is certainly true. Its being true, however, does not mean that trait theories of personality are incorrect. If they were traits, subjects could observe the signs and make the inferences, just as they can if there are not traits. Attribution theory indeed is rather like mental factor analysis, which is better done on a computer.

An important part of social psychology is concerned with attitudes and, therefore, with the measurement of attitudes. One of the crucial questions is to what extent attitudes cause behaviour.

In this section of this chapter I shall examine attitude measurement, as practised in social psychology in order to ascertain whether any reliance can be placed on the findings and theories based upon such measurement.

Attitude measurement

The first difficulty before measurement can even begin arises from the meaning of attitude and it is no simple matter to define precisely what is meant by the term although it is widely used. I think that a workable first approximation is the definition adopted by Cattell – a tendency to act in a particular way to a situation (1957). It is, however, not only a tendency because it results in action from time to time even if the action is no more than saying something. Cattell actually has attempted to give an operational definition of attitude, which is suitable for research and this highlights many of the difficulties with more traditional definitions. This paradigm is as follows. In these circumstances (the stimulus situation) I (organism) want so much (interest, need) to do this (goal or course of action) with that (object concerned with action). This implies that for understanding an individual's attitude, data are required concerned with the nature of the course of action, the intensity of interest in the course of action and, in most circumstances, the object involved in the course of action.

This is a somewhat unusual approach to defining attitudes and one which is rather different from that usually used, as we shall see, in social psychology. However, it is far more capable of embracing the full richness of what is normally meant by attitude and by examining this definition in detail, some of the inevitable weaknesses and flaws in the standard social psychological approach to the measurement of attitudes will be clarified. This is not to say, however, that Cattell's approach based upon this definition is itself adequate, something that will also be carefully scrutinized later in this chapter.

First, however, I shall examine Cattell's definition to see how it deals with the more usual notions of attitudes. A few examples will make the matter clear. Attitudes to nuclear bombs are a good current example. People generally can be placed on a continuum running from violent opposition to very strong support. Thus at one pole we find the CND supporter who considers nuclear warfare morally reprehensible, that nuclear explosions will destroy the world which would be unfit for living, were there anybody alive, that nuclear bombs are no deterrent because none will dare to use them. At the other pole lie those who believe that it is better to be dead than red, that without a bomb, Russia would invade the West, that our forty years of peace are due to the nuclear armoury. Wars are prevented by the bomb. Thus Cattell's paradigm becomes, for the nuclear supporter, in the world today, even in time of war, I am determined to build up a stock of nuclear weapons and use them if required against any enemy in order to prevent Russian or any other domination.

This example demonstrates how a typical attitude, as measured by social psychologists, will fit the definition that I am proposing. The social psychological approach which tends to polarize attitudes as verbal statements for or against something is also quite appropriate. However, as Cattell argues, many attitudes are not at all encapsulated by for or against. For example attitudes to a woman or man invoking love or hate cannot be reduced to for or against. Cattell's operational definition takes on a whole variety of attitudes to which this particular bipolarity, for or against, is simply irrelevant.

This is the background to my examination of attitude measurement in social psychology. As Eiser point out, attitude is perhaps the most frequently used term in social psychology, often used so vaguely as to render it useless. However, Eiser argues that 'the single most important function which scales of attitude measurement seek to achieve is to compare people in terms of their positive or negative evaluation of a given attitude object' (1980). Measuring scales are essentially summary statements to the effect that a person 'has a more or less favourable or unfavourable attitude towards the attitude object'. Thus then there is no doubt that social psychology, as propounded by Eiser, who is a leading figure in attitude measurement, seeks to place people on a favourable–unfavourable continuum, for or against. Cattell's earlier description of social psychology still holds. If this is the aim of attitude measurement it is already doomed to failure, even if it is done superlatively well. One final example will clarify this awful conceptual flaw. Attitudes to women, in general as distinct from any particular individual, include ideas such as: women are biologically different from men; in Western culture, at least, women have different attitudes from men; women are more flexible than men; women are less rational, more intuitive than men; women are more empathetic than men; women value individuals more than abstract principles compared with men; women are less aggressive than men; women are the basis of the family; women are emotionally supportive; women should be at home; women are no different from men; women have been exploited by society; high achievement in the arts and science is beyond women; women should remain quietly in the background; women should not tempt men. These statements certainly exemplify some, if not all, aspects of attitudes to women. There is no way in which a summary statement could be made either for or against.

One possible argument that social psychology could use is to allow that some attitudes are less amenable to measurement than others, but that many attitudes still fall along a continuum that is essentially for and against so that in these, the majority of cases, attitude measurement is perfectly possible. To evaluate this argument I shall now scrutinize the most commonly used techniques of attitude measurement.

Thurstone's method specifically aims to locate a person's attitude on the continuum of favourable–unfavourable towards a specific object. Individuals are presented with statements relevant to the attitudes and they have to indicate whether they agree or disagree with them. These statements have previously been rated by judges on an eleven-point scale of favourable–unfavourable in respect of the object of the attitude. A subject's score is the average rating of the statements with which he agrees. Of course all depends on the rating of the judges. Items on which there is considerable variance of ratings are not included in the scale and the rating for each item is the mean or median of the judges' ratings.

I hope that it is hardly necessary for me to point out that this method of scale construction is not without its problems. First of all it assumes that the eleven-point rating scales are equal intervals, that is, that a given difference on scale values reflects an equal difference in attitude, at any point in the scale. Such an assumption is by no means obvious. Even more important are the judges in this method of scale construction. Ideally, sufficient judges should be sampled so that all shades of opinion are covered otherwise the ratings will be hopelessly biased. Originally,

Thurstone had argued that the ratings could be regarded as absolute because judges were instructed to ignore their own views when they rated the statements. However, as a moment's reflection shows, this is impossible. Take the statement 'I think that Blacks should have the same education as Whites'. To a White South African this might seem highly favourable, to a Black Militant it would not be so classified. Attitudes are an integral part of one's values and personal identity, and objectivity in any real sense is impossible. Thus because the attitudes of the judges must affect the ratings these scale values must be regarded as relative to each other not absolute. This, therefore, creates a considerable problem with Thurstone scaling and renders comparability of scales impossible. Even if this is ignored there is still need for a wide sampling of judges. However there are simple practical problems with this and, as a result of all these difficulties, Thurstone scaling has tended to be replaced by Likert scaling.

Likert scales consist of statements, either obviously favourable or obviously unfavourable to the relevant attitude object, to which subjects have to respond on a five-point scale – strongly agree to strongly disagree. For negative items scoring is reversed so that five is received for strongly disagree. A subject's score is his total score on the items. This simple method is more reliable than Thurstone's, is far easier to construct and seems to correlate well with it.

For both types of scale items are often statements about the object found in newspapers or made in speeches. Thus any criticisms are common to both types of scale, although, as I have argued, Thurstone scales suffer further from the biases of judges and the logistics of sampling them.

I shall not mention again the criticism that the simple polarity of favourable–unfavourable is insufficient to conceptualize attitudes fully, even those to which superficially at least, such as Blacks or war, it might be held to apply. There are, however, yet more severe flaws in attitude measurement which I shall now point out. First, there is the problem of the veracity of the responses. In attitude questionnaires it is assumed that a subject is truthful if he agrees that 'women should be encouraged to work' and that 'men should take an equal share in child-rearing': since they have taken *any* share sales of disposable nappies have risen enormously. Indeed if men menstruated, pre-menstrual tension and pain would be things of the past. However, the individual who thus endorses it may be lying, because by so putting it he hopes to convince himself that the statement is true, if, for example, his partner strongly endorses the view. He may respond thus because, in his group, it is socially desirable so to do, and social desirability (the tendency to endorse a socially desirable item because of its social desirability) is a phenomenon which distorts all questionnaires. Sometimes subjects may sincerely believe that they have expressed their view yet when faced with the reality may realize that this is not so. Many a liberal parent has felt discomfort when their child proposed marriage to an 'unsuitable' individual, be it in terms of race or social class. In addition to this there are response tendencies, endorsing extremes or always choosing the middle category, which can create quite false results.

Here it must be noted that such strictures, although equally applicable to personality questionnaires do not distort them to the same extent. This is because the responses to individual items on questionnaires are not looked upon as accurate self-reports in the same way. Questionnaire items are chosen because they load on a factor which has some external validity. Thus virtually by definition these unwanted sources of variance cannot be influencing the results.

However, it is not simply that attitude questionnaires are assumed to be truthfully answered that causes considerable disquiet. In addition there is a further difficulty that there are unconscious determinants of behaviour which are not even allowed for in the attitude scales I have described. Thus simple statements about attitudes are far too crude to be useful. Let us take the example of attitude to Blacks. There can be little doubt that there are some unconscious determinants of our feelings in this instance. Many people project on to Blacks their own unacceptable impulses. Others, ashamed of their feelings of distaste, may overcompensate (sometimes called reaction formation). Others simply deny their feelings. All these problems mean that simple attitude scales cannot be sufficient. Such statements as may be made may be little more than rationalization, finding good excuses for what one wants to do.

For all these reasons, therefore, the idea that asking subjects to respond to simple statements can be an adequate measure of attitudes even when these are reduced to summaries – favourable or unfavourable towards an object – is somewhat ridiculous. If psychology were that simple, and all that had to be done was to count the agreements to statements, then why is it that we are so far from understanding attitudes and their relationship to behaviour, a problem that I will discuss later in this section.

In brief I have demonstrated that the standard social psychological approach to attitude measurement is hopelessly flawed: it conceptualizes attitudes in far too limited a fashion; it suffers from a variety of measurement errors; it ignores sources of bias and unconscious determinants of attitudes.

The important conceptual flaw was highlighted, it will be remembered, by Cattell's far more inclusive operational definition. Cattell and his colleagues over the years have attempted to develop tests based upon this theoretical approach. These tests, the Motivational Analysis Test (MAT) and its school equivalent, the SMAT, do purport to go deeper into the measurement of attitudes than recording disagreements or not with overt statements. These attempt to measure the drives underlying attitudes, and thus include unconscious aspects of attitude. Cattell has attempted further to develop objective tests which take into account the defences and other psychodynamic mechanisms that are found in clinical descriptions of personality (1957). In principle, therefore, the MAT would appear to overcome many of the objections I have made to the standard approach to attitude measurement. However, my own research into the validity of this test has cast considerable doubts on its ability to measure these underlying drives. Examination of the evidence adduced by Cattell and his colleagues shows that this, too, is far from conclusive. The principles and the statistical techniques which underpin the test are excellent but as yet more work is needed. It cannot with honesty be said that the MAT is a good measure of the drives which go to support an attitude.

From all this argument it is obvious that I consider that attitudes are not well measured in psychology, and thus I am hardly surprised that there is little evidence that behaviour can be predicted from attitudes. I think that in reality if we know what a person's attitude is, then we can predict behaviour. For example, if we know that a person feels Blacks are inferior, dirty and evil, it is nonsense to think that his behaviour will not confirm this attitude. Where this is not the case, then the measurement of attitudes must be wrong (and for the reasons which I have given, this is most likely). The reason I say that it is nonsense if the attitude is not confirmed by the behaviour stems from the meaning of the words 'feels' or 'believes', which could equally well have been used. These words entail the corresponding behaviour. This separates them from the (more behaviouristic) 'says' that . . . Notice that this is all that we know from attitude scales. We infer belief and feeling from statements and that in essence is what is wrong with simplistic attitude measurement. That is why attitudes fail to predict behaviour, and that is why, as I have argued in this chapter, better measurement is essential.

Eiser attempts to explain the discrepancy between the scores on attitude tests and behaviour in a different way. He argues that attitude scales, at least as generally used, tend to measure general attitudes, and his example is attitudes to the law, but the behaviour which is studied is often quite specific, and this he exemplifies by drunken driving. Thus he argues that low correlations would be found between attitudes to the law and convictions for drunken driving. In other words drunken driving is not related to a generalized attitude to the law breaking. Nor is it, he goes on, related to attitudes to causing physical injury, again an attempt to predict the specific from the general. These examples, he claims, do not allow us to argue that behaviour cannot be predicted from attitudes, only that specific behaviour cannot be predicted from a more general attitude which we had *presumed* (his italics) encompassed it. If, however, we examined attitudes to drunken driving, then we probably would find reasonable correlations.

This argument appears wonderfully convincing. Close scrutiny, however – a practice that appears to be foreign to experimental psychologists unless they do it as Nelson once did – reveals that it will not do. The 'presumes' in italics sounds entirely reasonable. In the field of psychometrics it is indeed a common error. For example it was assumed impulsivity was part of extraversion. Factor analysis reveals that this is not so and the scales can be cleaned up, impulsivity migrating over to psychoticism. In psychometrics the rule is very much to allow the data to tell their own story. However the attitudinal case is different. Take the example of attitude to law breaking. If attitude to law breaking has any meaning it must apply to breaking all laws. If not all laws then this means there is no such general attitude. If there is no general attitude, then possibly there is an attitude to groups of laws. If this is not the case then there must be an attitude to each separate law, but this is manifestly absurd. The point is that it makes no sense to say that a general attitude to law breaking does not apply to a particular law and that it was an error to presume it does so. It does so by definition. That it does not apply means either that there is no general attitude, as I have said, or that the measure of it is inadequate. The same argument applies to the attitudes to inflicting injury. Either there is a general law which must apply to drunken driving or there is not. Thus the failure to predict cannot be laid at the door of the difficulty of predicting the specific from the general. The failure must be due either to the fact that there is no general attitude or to measurement error.

I am dubious, too, about the meaning of the claim that if we want to predict drunken driving, a study of the attitudes to drunken driving would probably allow us to do so. As I have shown, attitude scales consist of statements about the attitudinal object to which subjects have to agree or disagree. Thus typical items would be: drunken driving should be heavily punished; drunken drivers should be banned for life; drunken driving is a crime; to kill somebody by drunken driving is murder; drunken driving is a dangerous peccadillo. Thus the contention becomes that there is a relationship between what people say about drunken driving, their views, opinions and feelings, and drunken driving itself. A positive correlation does not seem to be a particularly striking finding. Only lying and self-deception could make it otherwise.

I shall say no more about attitude measurement. I think that in general it is not well done because of the grossly simplistic approach to the problem. I am certain that no great weight should be attached to any of the findings.

Cognitive dissonance

I shall now examine, as a final aspect of social psychology, cognitive dissonance. Cognitive dissonance has been described as perhaps the most influential theory in social psychology so, although it is by no means new, it is clearly a salient area of the subject. Cognitive dissonance, in this theory, is said to occur after we have had to choose between two equally attractive courses of action. To overcome this dissonance, people re-evaluate the alternatives such that the chosen one becomes more attractive. This re-evaluation can either maximize the good aspects of the chosen one or the bad aspects of the rejected or both. Either way the tension or dissonance is reduced. In ordinary life cognitive dissonance is most often seen when we have to make a decision over buying a car. Cars are a particularly good example because after a house they are probably the most expensive article most people purchase and in the West there is an enormous variety with ostensibly little to choose between models. Apart from any emotional significance which cars may have, the choice is rarely flippant. My own choice exemplifies cognitive dissonance extremely well. I spent £10,000 on a Morgan. Compared with other similarly priced cars it is uncomfortable, noisy, draughty, awkward to drive and not particularly fast. There is thus a dissonance set up that I have spent a huge sum of money on a car that by these objective criteria is inferior to its alternatives. This dissonance could be dispersed by re-evaluating the others, but this is factually impossible, although to some extent I can re-evaluate the others by concentrating on their lack of individuality and character, and their modern plastic feel. Instead I concentrate upon certain Morgan traits, its heritage, the Morgan tradition, its beautiful lines and its hand-built character. This indeed is successful, and I do not feel that I have made a wrong choice. Thus I resolve the dissonance and there is no inconsistency in my purchase.

In the experimental studies of cognitive dissonance this process is labelled re-evaluation of the two alternatives, concentrating on the good aspects of the one and the bad aspects of the other. It also involves selective recall (of the best and worst sides), which has also been shown to be important in the resolution of dissonance. Two other methods of dealing with the problem are freedom of choice and persuading oneself that the consequences of the choice could not be foreseen. Freedom of choice hardly enters car buying although people with large families who might like a sporting vehicle can claim that they had to have an estate car and this will reduce dissonance on that score. If the car turns out truly terrible, it is possible to argue that nobody could have foreseen it would be so bad (all the reports were good) and again this may be helpful.

From this everyday example it is clear what cognitive dissonance is really about. Most people cannot hold dissonant cognitions in their mind. Therefore one of these cognitions (or both) has to be changed. There are many other examples of this resolution in everyday life. Thus public schools are extremely expensive and are, in some ways, overtly unpleasant – bullying by senior boys, cold baths, and so on. Thus to resolve the dissonance they are said to provide extremely good education – building the character and spirit in a way that state schools cannot hope to emulate. Indeed a common method of resolving dissonance is to become extremely keen on the object. Thus where there is vast enthusiasm cognitive dissonance must be suspected.

The experimental work on cognitive dissonance has confirmed these claims in general although it must be noted that the theory is somewhat vague as to how dissonance is likely to be resolved, that is it makes no prediction whether subjects will exaggerate the one or minimize the qualities of the other alternative. One interesting point is that cognitive dissonance can occur as a consequence of action. For example, if I am tempted by the appearance of some delicious fruit to buy South African produce, I can reduce the dissonance with my belief in anti-apartheid by letting myself believe that actually not buying such produce simply harms the people whom I wish to help. Another point which experimentalists have made much of is that if one does something which is contrary to one's beliefs for money the more one is paid the less shift in cognition there will be in order to reduce dissonance. This is an obvious prediction from the theory. If I can say I did it because I was paid so much that I could not refuse, even though it is against my beliefs, I do not have to change my beliefs in order that they may be consonant with my actions. However, if I have done it for virtually nothing, the only way to reduce dissonance is to change the beliefs.

I do not want to deny that dissonance theory has the stamp of truth. It does seem correct that people prefer to have a coherent belief system that fits together neatly and that if this is disturbed, some corresponding changes in beliefs and values are made to restore it. However the fact that dissonance theory cannot specify in advance what changes will occur considerably weakens its predictive power. Furthermore there is reason to think that dissonance reduction may be far more complex than the simple matter of changing cognitions. All the psychodynamic notions of defences can be seen as efforts to reduce dissonance. For example the daughter who is forced to look after her aging mother cannot accept her anger against her and changes it (by reaction-formation) to loving care but at considerable cost to the spirit, or (by displacement) is furious with her colleagues at work. As soon as all this is included in the theory, as in truth it should be, we can see that there is little new about dissonance theory. In brief it is true, as far as it goes, but it goes little further than many people go from their own experience of life. It cannot be regarded as an insightful step on the path of understanding.

Conclusions

What conclusions can be drawn from this examination of four important topics in social psychology? The Prisoner's Dilemma exemplifies for me all the worst aspects of experimental psychology. How studying so artificial a game could ever seriously be thought to contribute to knowledge about other topics defies belief. Careful scrutiny showed that belief was not defied. This research was arid, a peculiarly silly form of hermeneutics. Attribution theory I demonstrated was a careful delineation of how people make judgements about personality, basing them on observations and where these fail to explain, on implicit theories of human personality. There was little of interest or surprise here and much of it appeared to be self-evident. Attitude measurement was clearly flawed conceptually and even technically and the claims that the failure to predict behaviour from attitudes was due to the attempt to predict the specific from the general, I argued, did not withstand scrutiny. Finally, the claims of cognitive dissonance theory were found largely correct but so general as to be able to predict nothing.

From all these arguments it is clear that social psychology is little more than simply descriptive. It puts in more formal language what many, admittedly not all, would believe on the basis of their own experience. However, in reality it goes no further than common sense but it is common sense pompously expressed.

Chapter six

Cognitive science: Electrons or human beings?

In recent years, under the title of cognitive science, there have been numerous studies of information processing in both human beings and computers; many scholars in the field believe that these throw great light on human cognition. In some respects cognitive science is the modern, high technology equivalent of the cognitive models of memory which I discussed in Chapter 3. There seems little doubt that some of the putatively brightest young research workers are attracted into this field, which even in Great Britain is generously funded.

In this chapter I will discuss some of the recent work in order to see whether it is really concerned only with computers and their application to automatic perception and learning, or whether it tells us anything at all about human cognition. In other words is this work concerned ultimately with electrons or with human beings?

Brains and computers

As has been pointed out the first difficulty that has to be faced in this field is that the human brain, as a processing system, is different from a conventional computer. The computing elements in the brain operate in the millisecond range which is about a million times slower than current electrons. Since reaction times in most human performance are a few hundred milliseconds, it follows that must be approximately 100 computational time steps in solving recognition problems. This same limitation on computing also suggests that only simple signals can be sent from one neuron to another. In addition to all this the human information processing system, when compared with computers, is far more adaptable, tolerant of errors and context sensitive. The effortless recognition of different voices, accents and typefaces still defeats computers.

The relevance of this to computational modelling of human and artificial intelligence is that these neural constraints must be taken into account. As is argued in a symposium edited by Feldman (1985), it means that the brain cannot directly interpret some formal system such as a transformational grammar, for even if, as is most unlikely, transformational grammar became a theory of language, it will still be necessary to show how language is actually processed in the brain. What is necessary, therefore, in cognitive science studies, are formal systems which are coherent with the computational architecture of the human brain.

Some modern cognitive scientists are now working in this tradition so that their theories should both be computable and yet fit the human constraints. These scientists have been called the new connectionists and it is their work which I want to examine since, ostensibly at least, the problem of the simple processing differences between brains and computers will not be ignored by them.

The papers I will discuss are conveniently collected together in the symposium edited by Feldman (1985) to indicate the way in which this research is developing, and the promise it has for the future. It can be seen, therefore, that the symposium constitutes an ideal source for my purpose – the evaluation of this work for understanding human psychology. The symposium also has the advantage that it was deliberately written for non-specialists so that there is a minimum of programming and algebra (although I must say the papers are by no means simple). I will endeavour to make this difficult material comprehensible because shorn of the complex detail the problem is simple, namely whether the development of a system that will compute some decision or recognition process tells us anything at all about human beings. Although a priori the answer would appear to be negative, it is essential to scrutinize a few of these solutions before so damning and final an evaluation.

Parallel processing

Before I start to examine any of these individual papers, there is a general problem in the computer modelling of human cognition with which implicitly or explicitly all modern workers in this field are forced to deal. This is clearly stated in the article by Waltz and Pollack. They point out that computer scientists and cognitive psychologists who are attempting to develop computer models are limited by a conceptual framework of serial processing, which itself is a relic of the thirty year old framework of the von Neumann computer. This, to quote Waltz and Pollack, consisted of a Central Processing Unit connected to its passive array of memory by a small bundle of wires. It has been argued that conventional programming languages are high level versions of the von Neumann computer and the fact that until recent years most computer scientists believed that this was the only kind of computer rested on the fact that they believed this was the only kind of programming language. All this has led to the primacy of what might be called von Neumann thinking and attempts to develop other types of language have been hindered by this convention. The lack of efficient, effective programming along non-von Neumann principles has led to a serious intellectual weakness in thinking about new computer architectures. This argument on the deadening effects of what might be called conventional computer thinking (brilliant though this is) was proposed in 1977 by Backhus and, as I indicated, the studies which I am about to scrutinize are attempts to break this conventional mould.

The approach which most computer scientists have used to overcome the problem is to devise parallel processing models. Such models had been previously used in cognitive psychology but, under the constraint of von Neumann thinking, it had not been obvious how these could be implemented into a computer model. It should be pointed out at this juncture that some form of parallel processing seems essential to encapsulate all that goes on in complex human cognition such as understanding language where experimental studies indicate the necessity of interactions between letter recognition, word recognition and meaning – all difficult to achieve, in the manner of human cognition, without parallel processing being involved.

Waltz and Pollack, as we have seen, have clearly conceptualized the general problems of producing a computational model of understanding language and I shall now examine their attempt to do just that. I do not intend to describe their model in detail, which would be difficult to do without considerable technical discussion. However I hope to give readers the essence of the work, sufficient to be able to see to what extent it throws light on human cognition. In brief is this work relevant to human psychology or is it in fact clever computation?

The work of Waltz and Pollack

To understand language, as it is normally used, an individual has to integrate knowledge from many sources or systems: knowledge of word use, word order, phrase structure and knowledge of a real world, situations, events, roles and contents. Although each of these knowledge systems could be separately stored, a language processor which simply serially joined these together cannot effectively or realistically do this.

There are various well-known difficulties in understanding language which serial processing cannot adequately deal with. By adequately deal with I mean that when a serial solution is applied to the problems the delays taken before the system solves the problems are quite unlike human performance. It is in that sense that serial processing is seen to be inadequate. This applies to the solution of ambiguity in which backtracking or waiting and seeing to the end of the sentence will not just do. Similarly it applies to comprehension errors in which more obvious but anomalous meanings have to be changed. The example given by these authors is the 'astronomer married the star'. The fact that the authors of the paper find this example (which is not their own but from another psycholinguistic computer scientist) mildly amusing causes me to wonder whether their grasp of the subtleties of language is all it should be in those purportedly investigating the subject. It seems a hideous coincidence, but in many fields of psychology, psychologists are involved because of their own deficiencies. I am quite happy, I should add, that this arrow be pointed at me. Again the fact that double interpretations of sentences are not held simultaneously but rather we go from one to the other suggests parallelism rather than serialism. A final example of the necessity for the integration of knowledge, and hence parallel processing, is the ability of most people to understand non-grammatical language. Actually Waltz and Pollack make this point in an ungrammatical sentence: 'People are able to interpret non-grammatical language whether it is naturally occurring (due to poor grammar, foreign speakers, noise interference, self-corrections, etc.).' Is this a subtle form of semiotics or are these authors the stereotype of the illiterate numerate? They *appear* to conclude that this ability demands integration because meaningfulness and grammaticality are independently judged. However this final sentence is again ungrammatical and I am uncertain that this ability is as independent as they think.

All these phenomena indicate that serial processing, the passing of semi-complete results between processing components, will not do. Rather an interactive model is needed where all decisions are interdependent. Their model used two processes – spreading activation and lateral inhibitions. Spreading activation of the analogue kind involves distributing activation energy through a network based upon a mathematical function of the strength of connections. This system can become overloaded such that the whole network becomes uniformly activated. This can be damped down by lateral inhibition which spreads negative energy in the same way as the activation spreads positive energy. Thus in a network with weighted nodes and links and an iterative operation which recomputes the activation level of each node (based on its current value and that of its links and neighbours), an activating link between nodes will cause them to support each other while an inhibiting link will allow only one pair to remain active at a given time.

In the parsing model inhibiting links are placed between nodes which represent well-formed phrases with shared constituents; between nodes representing different lexical categories of the same word; between nodes representing different meanings of the same word. On the other hand, there are activation links between phrases and their constituents, between words and their different meanings, for example. Thus over several iterations, a coalition of nodes representing a consistent interpretation will dominate. This is the basic architecture of the system which is shown by Waltz and Pollack to be able to extract the correct meaning from ambiguous sentences, for instance 'the astronomer married the star', using context, syntax and various aspects of priming.

I have outlined the principles of this automatic parsing system which can extract sense from very simple ambiguous sentences, without going into the details of how the activation and inhibition of the nodes and links in the networks enable a sensible meaning to be extracted. However these details are not important for my question. Does this massively parallel parser throw light on the human comprehension of language?

I cannot think that it does. Even if it were perfectly able to mimic the human comprehension of language, there would be no necessity that human comprehension was based on an identical system. However, as it stands, this parser is hideously crude: it does extremely little of what a person does when reading. There is so much more to reading than disambiguating a few inane sentences. 'The sailor ate the submarine' seems the height of literary brilliance to these authors, so perhaps the connotations, implications, and suggestions of ordinary text bypass their minds long devoted to computers. Let me take an example from *The Wilt Alternative* – a by no means subtle comedy. My comments are in square brackets.

'I'd like to see a doctor,' he said with some difficulty.
'Have you broken something?' asked the woman.
'Sort of,' said Wilt, conscious that his conversation was being monitored
by a dozen other patients with more obvious but less distressing injuries.
[Wilt has cut his penis. This is in Britain an extremely embarrassing injury.
Penises are not talked about. How is this built into the parser? If
under penis, the network would be very large.]
'What do you mean, sort of?'
Wilt eyed the woman and tried to convey wordlessly that his was a condition
that required discretion. [We know that Wilt is embarrassed because of the
injury and this 'convey wordlessly' has many implications re the audience
monitoring them. Where is this in the parser?] The woman was clearly
obtuse. [How is the parser to link 'clearly' with the fact that she cannot
accept Wilt's need to see a doctor, when clearly obtuse makes good sense?
The model proposed would certainly misunderstand. If it did not,
its complexity would become gargantuan.]
[A later point in the book.] The sister had picked up an aerosol can, 'Just
a mild disinfectant and freezer. I'll spray it on first and you won't
feel the little prick.' [There the prick refers to the hypodermic not the
small penis Wilt might have. The parser will give the correct meaning, but
the second implication, suppressed by lateral inhibition, will not appear.]

In conclusion this model parser may make simplistic machine translation possible, but it sheds no light on the human case. This is electronics not psychology. It would appear highly unlikely that the human system resembled this network. Although, as I argued, even if the system was able to comprehend exactly as do human beings, there is no necessity that it is the same, that possibility must be carefully considered. Thus it is not the case that all artificial intelligence systems can be automatically condemned as unlike the human case. Rather there is need to show that they are similar. If however, as with this automatic parser, it is quite clear that there is little similarity in performance, then the conclusion becomes obvious.

Recogniton of origami ducks

I will next examine briefly a study by Sabbah (1985) of a computational model for the recognition of origami objects which uses a connectionist approach, a term which is synonymous with massively parallel processing. As was the case with the automatic parser, discussed in more detail, a network of the critical features in the recognition of origami objects is set up – shapes, rays, lines, edges, L-joints, T-joints and C-joints for example. The parameters defining these terms are built into the network. Then an evidence integration formula is developed taking into account the activation level in the network.

The parallel processing approach eliminates a weakness of the older serial approach where, for example, the search for 'a parallel line' could lead to poor recognition, because the model was trapped by local maxima at the expense of the global optimum. Furthermore, because parallel processing allows the communication of partial results, there is a vast reduction in the total number of units which have to be examined at any one time, a major problem with the serial processing approach. With these advantages compared with the von Neumann computer, this system was able to recognize perfect origami figures but not figures with noised, incomplete and occluded input. This is certainly an impressive result and such recognition has proved difficult to produce in artificial intelligence studies.

Sabbah is modest about this work and he acknowledges a number of problems and the need for extending this approach. First, he admits that extensions of this model are necessary to even approximate recognition of objects in the real world. Complex three-dimensional shapes undergoing arbitrary three-dimensional transformations have to be represented and programmes to do this are under development, although problems of motion and non-rigid objects have not even been included at this stage. Nor have other sources of restraining information, such as colour, texture or shading, been incorporated into the network. However as more of these sources of information are included in the network, the problems in reaching a convergent solution become increasingly difficult. This information has to be independently computed in a parallel processing system, yet has to be present at the right time which is by no means simple to arrange.

There is yet another considerable difficulty, as Sabbah points out. Parallel processing does not eliminate the combinatorial explosion of possibilities of underconstrained search. For example if faces are to be mapped on to origami ducks, the number of connections is enormous (any one face can be mapped to a huge number of ducks). This causes activation of a very large number of units, which resembles random spreading activation and is a form of combinatorial explosion. To relieve this, additional levels of hierarchy can be made but at a cost – an increase in the number of units which is itself a problem. The solution appears to be, as Sabbah argues, to incorporate a mechanism for selective attention, first to shape, and then to other aspects of the field.

Finally, Sabbah argues that a system such as this might allow the possibility of two types of learning – learning specific instances and learning the abstract concept. Of course, how to extract the optimal representation that captures the abstraction is still a mystery in computing terms.

As I indicated Sabbah makes no inflated claims about this research which is in fact an impressive foray into artificial vision using parallel processing techniques. Nevertheless, it is clear that it cannot perform in any way that a human being does and that the program will be enormously complex if it is ever so to do. There can be little confidence on the basis of these results that anything about the organization of human visual processes could be learned. Again it must be concluded that this paper is a further example of research shedding light on the visual capabilities of computers rather than human beings.

McClelland has an interesting paper in this same collection where he makes some important points about the models I have discussed which, I think, confirm my view that they cannot be informative about human information processing. Activation network models utilize hard-wired connections between nodes. This means that there is considerable reduplication of connections which is highly cumbersome when, as is the case with understanding language, a huge amount of information has to be processed. To overcome this difficulty McClelland describes a mechanism, the connection information distributor (CID) which allows the connections within a network to be programmed, thus eliminating the need for hard-wiring and its consequent duplication of information. I do not intend to describe the details of this mechanism, which appears to me to be of a horrible complexity, but I am not a computer scientist. It has not been fully implemented and in any case deals so far only with four-lettered words. However, the principle is important because the CID, or any other similar structure, allows network models and all the advantages of parallel processing and the integration of different aspects of the information, essential for comprehension, with a small computational demand. To what extent this system can be implemented for more complex and realistic tasks remains to be seen. Nevertheless, this whole paper demonstrates that the state of the art is not advanced at present, that workers are still searching for the best approach even to simple problems of comprehension, that this search reflects difficulties and problems in computing rather than in human beings and that any extrapolation to human behaviour is quite unwarranted.

There is only one other paper in this symposium which I shall examine because this utilizes a different approach to the difficulties which beset computing models. The papers which I have ignored are not inferior to those which I have discussed but from the viewpoint of this book, they add no further information. They are essentially about computers.

Boltzmann Machine learning

Ashley, Hinton, and Sejnowski discuss Boltzmann Machine learning. A Boltzmann Machine is 'a parallel computational organization that is well suited to constraint satisfaction tasks [searches] involving large numbers of "weak" constraints'. A 'strong' constraint is one which must be satisfied by any solution. A 'weak' constraint is one which incurs a cost if violated. The quality of a solution is thus judged by the costs of violating the constraints.

In perceptual interpretation this total cost represents the implausibility of the interpretation.

The Boltzmann Machine consists of *units*, primitive computing elements, which are interconnected by bi-directional *links*. A link is either *on* or *off* its state depending on a probabilistic function of the states of its neighbouring units and the *weights* on its links to them. These weights can take on positive or negative values. If a unit is on, the system accepts; if off, it rejects some elementary hypothesis about the domain. The weight on a link represents a weak constraint about two hypotheses. A positive weight indicates that the two hypotheses tend to support each other. A negative weight suggests both should be rejected. Link weights are symmetric.

The global state of this network can be assigned a number which reflects the energy of the state. The aim of the system is to minimize this energy – the less it is the fewer violations of the weak constraints have been made. Some of the units can be forced or 'clamped' in particular states to represent a particular input, and the system will find the minimum energy configuration compatible with this input.

These authors have produced an algorithm to reach this minimum energy configuration, but the most interesting aspect of the Boltzmann Machine is that it leads to a domain-independent learning algorithm which modifies the connection strengths between units in such a way that the whole network develops an internal model which captures the underlying structure of its environment. As Ashley and his colleagues argue (1985), many workers in the field of artificial intelligence have abandoned the search for such an algorithm, the Eldorado of Computing. To test this algorithm an encoding problem was used in which two systems have to communicate their states to each other, for example two groups of units V_1 and V_2 represent two systems: each group has v units, either on or off, so there are v different states of each group. V_1 and V_2 are connected to H (a group of h units) with $h<v$. The learning algorithm allows the formation of a set of distributed representations which does reflect the states of the system.

As Ashley and his colleagues point out, in the Boltzmann Machine units reach 'eternal equilibrium' and the relative probability of being in two global states will follow the Boltzmann distribution which is closely related in its properties to information theory and it is this property which makes this machine so interesting and so full of potential for computational models of cognition. I mention the Boltzmann Machine because it seems that this approach based on the statistical mechanical approach to thermodynamics may enable more complex representations of the environment, than are required by encoding problems, to be built up. At present, however, it is highly speculative and its relationship to human cognitive processes can be no more than speculation. What can be concluded from this scrutiny of some recent papers in the field of computational models of cognition, papers which, as I have shown, are regarded as good examples of how the field is developing, papers moreover which have eschewed serial models which would rule them out of court as regards extrapolation to the human case?

First, as I have made clear, it would be quite wrong to attempt to argue that any of the models proposed here is such as could plausibly be thought to resemble the human process. This can be said with confidence because all these are so limited as to what they can do: to recognize an origami duck, even upside down, does not convince me that this is the system which governs the eye that can spot an eagle at 1,000 yards.

In effect this argument means that only when the human performance is precisely mimicked could we even feel that the system might be the same. But this raises the question of how we could ever be sure a computer model was the same as the human case. I think the only evidence that would be at all convincing is to find those examples where the computer model fails or gives unexpected results. If this occurred in the human case, then this could be regarded as good evidence certainly for the similarity (if not the identity) of the system. Similarly, human beings could be tested and where their performance was unexpected, there the computing model could be examined. At present, however, we are far from examples of this kind, at least in the field of knowledge representation. Thus I believe that these findings tell us more about electrons than human beings and that this field will only possibly become insightful when it is far more sophisticated.

A colleague suggested that my arguments in this section of the chapter were somewhat unfair because the authors of these papers had highly specific aims and I had chided them for failing to make more general points. For example, he argued that Waltz and

Pollack had not tried to tackle comprehension of English but to produce an algorithm that would parse. It was possible to parse an entirely artificial language (without meaning) and they had succeeded in this limited aim. This may well be true but it emphasizes and makes my point, namely that experimental psychology is content to deal with the trivial. To explicate 'marry a star' cannot rank high on the scale of human aspiration and that it is unlikely to be useful in the understanding of much comprehension even at a later stage of research is clear.

While universities and other institutions of education give the seal of approval to projects which are essentially small scale and trivial, and while they train people in such futile endeavours, real intellectual progress is impossible. It is an irony that universities, which are claimed to be institutions where ideas are valued, should almost deliberately thus exclude them.

My colleague also made a point which strongly supports my claim that much of what masquerades as science in psychology is nothing more than a defence against emotion and feeling. The whole chapter, he argued, was ruined because it was too passionate. Now I do not have to point out, I hope, the logical error in this statement that passion implies unreason, that only what is boring can be good science. Certainly that *must* be the belief of most writers of both books and papers. However, as I have shown throughout this book, low quality thought can certainly be found in papers of unsurpassing tedium. No, passionate writing suggests emotion – a dreadful evil. There can be little doubt that both these arguments confirm the gloomy truth of this book, that experimental psychology is a defence against feeling.

The work of Marr

I will now examine the work of Marr (1982) who has set out a computational approach to vision which is highly considered in its field. Indeed many experimental psychologists might cite Marr's work as an example of how experimental psychology can truly contribute to human knowledge and understanding, thus, in their opinion, rebutting the thesis of my book.

Marr argued that despite the success of physiologists in the study of vision, for example the discovery of cells mediating hand-detection in the cortex and the work on single cells involved in edge detection, this reductionist approach to perception had not proceeded beyond that point. Perception could not be thus explained. This ultimate failure, Marr agues, could be laid at the door of both neurophysiology and psychophysics, both of which were missing out something of great importance to a real understanding of perception. This missing element was explanation since neurophysiology and psychophysics are descriptive, the former of the behaviour of cells, the latter of subjects. Neither discipline attempted to answer the question, which is clearly central to visual perception, of what the visual cortex does.

To answer this question Marr himself migrated from the physiology of vision to artificial robotic vision at MIT with Minsky, maestro of machine intelligence. Apparently in the 1960s, when this work first began, it was believed that machine perception would be easy, a view which turned out to be illusion.

One approach was to use blind empiricism, simply producing algorithms which appeared to work, for example in edge detection. This, according to Marr, was not fruitful. A second approach was to simplify the visual world of the robot and to restrict it to white cubes on a black background or, as in the example in this chapter, to origami ducks. This, at least, clarifies what the problems of machine perception really are, although unfortunately it is not useful for providing the answers to even slightly more complex problems; an origami wren would defeat the program, let alone a grebe. Needless to say, the normal effortless perceptual skills of people in everyday life are not thus illuminated.

However, a third approach, Marr argues, did form the basis of successful machine perception. These studies are important not because they really illuminated human perception, but because of the way they were formulated. One example was the retinex theory of colour vision which regarded colour as a perceptual approximation to reflectance. This suggests a clear computational process – the separation of reflectance from variation in illumination. Since the latter is usually gradual and the former sharp, filtering out slow charges allows reflectance to be isolated. An algorithm was developed to do this, such that this study incorporated both what is to be compiled and how it is to be done, together with an analysis of the kind of algorithms that could do it – all the basic requirements of artificial vision. Similarly important was the set of equations that were developed by Horn, allowing shape to be derived from shading, relating image intensity to surface geometry.

These experiments, Marr argues, highlight what was missing from earlier work. There must be an additional level of understanding in which the character of the perceptual processing tasks are understood, and this understanding is itself an information processing task. Without this there can be no real understanding of the function of the individual neurons that have been shown to be involved in perception.

Such a formulation, Marr writes, enables the investigation of the information processing underlying perception to be rigorous. It is then possible, if explanations are separated into different levels, to make explicit statements about what is being computed, and why it is computed. Furthermore, theories may be constructed concerning the efficiency or functional excellence of what is being computed. Thus, the *ad hoc* element of empirical heuristic programming is removed, replaced 'by the solid foundations on which a real subject can be built'. This approach, the formulation of the missing element and the notions of how it may be supplied, is the basis of the integrated approach which constitutes Marr's distinctive contribution.

To understand the contribution of Marr to the study of vision, two terms – process and representation – require explication. A *representation* is a formal system for making explicit certain entities or types of information together with a specification of how the system does this. An example of this would be the various systems for representing numbers. In the Arabic system are contained the rules for descriptions of numbers (in multiples of the power of ten). A *description* is the result of using the representation to describe a given entity. Which representation one chooses affects what one can be done: for example, as Marr argues, the Arabic representation of number makes it easy to see whether a number is a power of ten; the binary representation is similarly easy for powers of two and vice versa. Roman numbers are difficult to multiply and so on.

We must now examine what Marr means by process, a term of enormous breadth and one which for the purposes of his discussion Marr restricts to its application in information processing machines. I shall use his example, a cash register, because it is particularly clear. There are, Marr argues, three levels necessary for understanding a cash register. The most abstract level is that concerned with *what* the register does and *why*. The answer to the first question is arithmetic (addition). Thus the theory of addition must be mastered. As to why, it is necessary to demonstrate that in the necessities of purchasing, addition is the requisite operation. All this Marr calls the computational theory of the register. In the theory of visual processes the task is to derive properties of the world from images of it.

The second level of the analysis of a process involves two things: a representation for the input and the output of the process and an algorithm by which the transformation can be effected. In the cash register input and output representations are both numbers. This is not always or even usually so. Thus, for example, in Fourier transforms time is input and frequency output. This second level of analysis specified how the process is carried out. Marr points out with respect to this level of analysis that there can be a wide choice of representations and this can affect the selection of a particular algorithm and that even for one representation several algorithms may be possible.

The third level is that of the device in which the process is to be realized. Important here is the fact that the same algorithm can be implemented in entirely different ways. Thus a child doing sums may use the same algorithm as the cash register.

Each of these three levels is necessary for a complete understanding of any process and hence they have their place in the comprehension of perceptual processes. However, since these levels are only loosely related some phenomena may be explicable at only one or two levels. In perception it is fairly clear at what level explanation should be sought (and much confusion is created, Marr argues, by trying to explain phenomena at the wrong level). For example, neuroanatomy is tied to the third level, the physical realization of the process. Psychophysics is related to the second algorithmic level.

Marr illustrates the value of his hierarchical analysis by claiming that it helps assess the validity of various objections to computational models. Thus one objection is that the brain is quite different from a computer because one is parallel, the other serial. This, of course, is the objection that I have accepted in this chapter by concentrating upon massively parallel systems. Marr argues that the distinction is at the level of algorithm and is not at all fundamental since anything written in parallel can be rewritten serially. 'The distinction, therefore, provides no grounds for arguing that the brain operates so differently from a computer that a computer could not be programmed to perform the same tasks.' Expressed in precisely those words, Marr is correct. However, the argument is unsound in principle. This can be shown by referring to the third level. If the computer program is serial, it may require such massive amounts of storage of information that, given the speed of *neuronal transmission* (the third level) the process would be inordinately slow. Thus the human process could not resemble the computer process. This is the meaning of the objection that the brain is different from the computer. Reference to the third level makes the point. Reference to the second level fails to support the objection, but this does not nullify it as Marr suggests.

Despite this somewhat unfair use of his model, Marr argues that the algorithms necessary for perception are far more likely to be understood by understanding the nature of the problem to be solved – the top level, the computational theory – than by examining the mechanisms (hardware or neurones) in which they are embodied. The importance of computational theory, *vis-à-vis* algorithms, runs through all processing including, for example, the relation of linguistics to artificial intelligence. Chomsky's theory of transformational grammar is a true computational theory, specifying *what* has to be done rather than how it is to be done, a second level problem.

So far, I have summarized some of the main concepts and assumptions which underlie Marr's approach to vision which he describes as representational framework for vision conceived as producing a useful description of the world from images of it, an image in this case being a representation. In this definition much turns upon the meaning of useful. In the case of the house fly, the system serves the needs of the fly well, but it yields little objective information about the world. However, man is not a fly and the question becomes, according to Marr, one of the kind of information delivered by vision and also the kind of representation.

Marr's answers to this question were based on clinical cases of disturbed vision in which it became obvious, from certain types of aphasia, that the representation of the shape of an object is quite separate from the representation of its use and purpose. In other words vision tells us about shape, space and spatial arrangements. From such clinical cases Marr decided that the quintessential purpose of vision was to derive a representation of shape.

To achieve this end a sequence of representations seemed necessary starting with descriptions that could be obtained straight from an image, but that allowed subsequent recovery of more detailed information. First, the geometry of the visible surfaces has to be described, for example stereopsis, shading, contours. However, such description is unsuited to recognition because too much depends upon the vantage point of the observer. The description has to become object rather than viewer centred. In Marr's information processing account there are three represent-ational stages: the primal sketch which explicates the two-dimen-sional image; the two-and-a-half dimensional sketch which expli-cates the orientation and rough depth of the visible surfaces but in a viewer centred framework. Finally, there is the three-dimen-sional model representation which places the object in an object-centred frame, giving the three-dimensional structure and its organization together with a description of its surface qualities.

What Marr essentially has achieved is to be able to formulate with some precision some computational processes which allow machine vision. However, as his arguments about serial and parallel processing indicate, it is by no means certain that human beings process information in this way when they perceive the world. Even if they did some important questions remain unansw-ered. Thus this work explains the mechanics of vision, what happens when we see. However, this system, interesting and diffi-cult to elucidate as it may be, could be regarded as a given when we come to think about the problems of vision. Let me take an example. If I see Margaret Thatcher shot by a gunman and a Marr programmed robot standing by me in the room sees the same event, are the effects the same on robot and me? What is interesting to the human psychologist is the content of vision; what is seen, rather than how it is seen. In this respect despite its intellectual brilliance, this work by Marr typifies the mechanistic approach to man which ultimately is trivial, in terms of the important problems described in this book. Of course, the same argument applies to all computer models of vision and meaning, such as I have discussed in this chapter. Until robots can feel and have emotions their information processing, however like the human case, will never throw light on human behaviour. For we do have feelings and these cannot be separated from anything we do. Alas this work on cognitive science tells us little about man.

Chapter seven

Animal psychology

In this chapter I shall examine studies conducted on animals from the viewpoint of their contribution to the understanding of human beings. Immediately this raises a difficulty which, we have seen, runs through other branches of psychology which I have discussed: namely that psychologists, often but not always, for the best of reasons, study something other than what they are truly interested in. A notorious example was the Prisoner's Dilemma which I demonstrated could not in fact stand for anything other than itself unless one were to include other similarly pointless games. In the case of animal psychology the gap appears, to me at least, even more glaring. To extrapolate from animals to man a priori seems absurd. Thus I think it is necessary for animal psychologists to demonstrate that such extrapolation is justified or at least attempt to offer some persuasive line of argument.

My argument that such extrapolation needs justification is not dissimilar to my misgivings about artificial intelligence and computational models of man. Let me exemplify briefly this somewhat obvious case. Suppose I were to study determinants of vocalization in the lion. It would be surprising if these were the same for a mouse, a whale, or a worm (which cannot actually vocalize anyway). It is certain that such findings would not apply in the human case. Few other organisms exhibit that narcissistic love of their own voices. Indeed it is generally accepted in animal psychology that extrapolation from species to species, even species that are closely related, is dangerous. Thus how extrapolations from animals to man can be justified seems difficult to argue.

There seems little doubt that genetically the higher apes are, of all living organisms, the closest to man. However despite their similar appearance, their stereoptic vision and their opposable thumbs, there remains (*pace* Washo and colleagues) an enormous divide – the possession of language.

I am prepared to assert (although I will bring evidence to uphold this point) that possession of language makes the behaviour of man radically different from that of animals. Some of our behaviour is verbally controlled. If I decide to have a holiday and come back on Wednesday to continue this book, I am highly likely to do so. Without language such long-term planning is impossible. This is a simple example of what is so blindingly obvious that I am embarrassed to have to write it, yet it appears to be necessary. Important laws of learning have been derived from the behaviour of dogs, rats and pigeons and have been held to apply to man to such an extent that these laws have been invoked in the treatment of neurosis and psychosis. In yet another branch of animal psychology, ethology, the observation of animals in their natural environment, some of the principles have been claimed to be relevant to human behaviour, although here the point has been less dogmatically argued than was the case with theories of learning. The other and more recent field of animal study is sociobiology. This asserts that animal, and ultimately human behaviour, can be best seen as an effort to maximize the life of one's genes. Thus the urge to self-defence and to protect one's children, to fight for food and territory: all can be explicated by invoking this basic drive.

It is quite clear that the advocates of these branches of psychology who claim that human behaviour can be understood in the light of their findings are not so stupid as to have overlooked my basic objection to their work. This is especially so since some of the best known figures in the study of behaviour in general are from these branches – Skinner, Pavlov, Lorenz, Tinbergen and Wilson.

For these reasons, therefore, I shall examine some of the key concepts and experiments in these fields in order to see whether my initial objection can be upheld. This, again, is the claim that the possession of language (of an advanced kind) makes the behaviour of man incomprehensible if its role not only in planning but in the expression and experience of emotions is not fully taken into account. This can never be done when inferences based upon the behaviour of animals are employed.

Sociobiology

First, I will examine sociobiology, a branch of biology that has been to a large extent created by the Harvard zoologist Wilson, in a number of widely read and cited publications (Wilson 1975 and 1978). The essence of their arguments is that all behaviour is purposive: to perpetuate an individual's genes. The survival of the gene is the universal linch-pin of behaviour. The brain exists because it promotes the survival and multiplication of the genes that direct its assembly. The human mind is a device for survival and reproduction and reason is just one of its techniques. The point here that reason, the supreme good of Platonic philosophy and eighteenth-century philosophy, is only one of the techniques reflects the view of the opening paragraph of *Sociobiology* (Wilson 1975), namely that the emotional control centres of the hypo-thalamus and limbic system flood the consciousness with emotion – hate, love, guilt, and fear – and these are the basis of ethics, and this basis has evolved through natural selection. However, sociobiologists assert, natural selection is not about the survival of the individual, who is but a vehicle for genes, but the survival of genes. Thus even the intuited standards of good and evil, the world of philosophy, are ultimately to be conceptualized as devices for the perpetuation of DNA.

What sociobiology has done, therefore, is to examine the social behaviour of man and other organisms in the light of this view-point and it claims that the organization, the structure and nature of human social behaviour are consonant with this view. It also asserts that the organization of non-human groups can be so explained, although this aspect of the theory is not so relevant to the thesis of my book, which, of course, is concerned with the understanding of human behaviour.

There are several points about this claim which need discussion. First, it is quite clear that sociobiology is not trivial in the way that I have shown so much of experimental psychology to be. It deals directly with the most fundamental aspects of human behaviour. Its claim, for example, that morality is biologically programmed into the brain is certainly striking. Thus Wilson is quite unequivocal about the influence of the limbic system and the hypothalamus. In *On Human Nature*, Wilson writes 'innate censors and motivations exist in the brain that deeply and unconsciously affect our ethical premises: from these roots, morality evolved as instinct' (1978). Again, 'The oracle resides in the deep emotional centres of the brain, most probably within the limbic system.' This argument, which certainly reflects his definition of sociobiology as the systematic study of the biological basis of all forms of social behaviour, that morality has biological origins, is clearly of considerable importance. It is also contra-intuitive, since most psychologists and indeed philosophers would see morality as a function of learning within a given culture.

A second point, which sociobiologists all take up, is that the thesis that all behaviour is aimed at the perpetuation of an individual's genes seems, at first glance and in the human case, to be false. Altruistic acts, leading, in war, to death which was virtually inevitable, would seem to contradict the argument.

There is, furthermore, a third more general difficulty. This concerns the evidence on which the sociobiological arguments rest. In the original *Sociobiology*, for example, many non-human societies are described and cited and these are held to illustrate the claim. Similarly, in the human case anthropological evidence is cited. Now few of us are polymaths enough to know all this evidence well. Opponents of sociobiology cite counter-claims and there can be little doubt that much anthropological evidence is suspect (certainly different accounts of the same societies can be found). The whole problem of evidence, and indeed what would constitute positive or negative evidence, is a real difficulty with this theory.

In the remainder of this section on sociobiology I will evaluate its claims in these two important spheres of behaviour, morality generally, and altruism as a specific and apparently counter example. Finally, I shall discuss the more general problem of what can be predicted from sociobiological theory.

Religion

In most cultures morality is institutionalized as religion or by its modern secular equivalents, the political philosophies of Mao or Marx for example. Thus it is instructive to examine what Wilson has to say about religion to which he devotes a chapter in *On Human Nature*. He begins, 'The predisposition to religious belief is the most complex and powerful force in the human mind and in all probability an ineradicable part of human nature.' The first point to note is the use of the word 'predisposition'. Thus sociobiologists assume that there is a predisposition to believe; that is, man is made such that he will believe. This statement assumes what in fact sociobiologists seek to demonstrate – that there is a biological basis to human behaviour. There is another built-in assumption to this opening sentence, namely that this 'predisposition' is the 'most complex and powerful force in the human mind'. Scientifically, I regret to say this is nonsense. Forces of the mind have never been measured along any dimension. Thus the claim that this disposition (which has never been demonstrated) is more complex or more powerful than any other force has no meaning. It is no more than the ordinary rhetoric of lay thinking. I might say that sexuality or maternal love or love of one's country is the most powerful force in the human mind. Until forces can be measured such statements should be avoided. However, if Wilson means that religious belief (not the predisposition) is a powerful force in the human mind, few would disagree. Such a statement needs no sociobiology to support it. It is, alas, everywhere evident – Israel, Lebanon, Northern Ireland, Iraq, Ireland, Korea, Vietnam.

Leaving aside those difficulties, this richly assumptive first sentence concludes that the predisposition is probably ineradicable. Of course, as it stands, Wilson is correct. If a person believes it supports his position. If a person does not believe it is the belief, not the predisposition, that has been eradicated. Thus the only evidence that could support his theory is in distant evolutionary time. If in every society, none believed despite every possible environmental encouragement, the predisposition, which might still exist, would have to be said to be weak! So much for the first sentence which as science is highly dubious and best ignored.

Religious belief is an anthropological universal. What arguments does Wilson use to demonstrate its biological basis? These can be summarized. Religion is difficult to eradicate and has not retreated before scientific knowledge either in the USA or Russia. Nor has humanism fared better than science in the battle. Thus advanced societies exist in a kind of schizophrenia where knowledge is combined with a value system which that knowledge is destroying. However, this paradox can be understood when religious practices are mapped ·on to the two sociobiological dimensions – genetic advantage and evolutionary change.

Religions, it is asserted, are subject to cultural Darwinism. Those that gain adherents grow, the others disappear, and thus they evolve in directions that help the practitioners. Because the benefits must accrue to the group as a whole, they are gained partly by altruism and partly by exploitation. Furthermore, the key learning rules and their ultimate genetic motivation are probably unconscious because religion is the process by which individuals are persuaded to subordinate immediate self-interest to the interest of the group. If we accept these claims for the moment, the question now involves the unconscious processes giving rise to religious beliefs which help individuals in a society: what is their biological basis?

According to Wilson natural selection for religious beliefs operates at three levels: at the surface ecclesiastical selection, rituals and convictions selected by religious leaders, of which the results are culturally transmitted, thus accounting for cultural variations in religious practices. Variations in religious practice from society to society stem from learning not genes. These practices are put to an evolutionary test. If they weaken society they die out or change. As all this goes on, gene frequencies are changing.

The sociobiological hypothesis is that some gene frequencies are changed in constant ways by ecclesiastical selection. Genes, it is argued, constrain the maturation and learning rules of various behaviours. Examples of these involved also in religion are incest taboos and trance induction. Thus ecclesiastical choices are influenced by genes and influence them. Religious practices which enhance survival will propagate the genes that favour acquisition of these practices.

What evidence does Wilson bring to support this interaction between genes and culture in understanding religion? He regards sacred rituals as strongly confirming his case, for they mobilize and display primitive societies in ways that are directly biologically advantageous – for example displaying the strength and wealth of tribes. Military parades and Potlach ceremonies are two illustrations, one from primitive, the other from modern highly technological societies. In addition rituals, it is claimed, regularize relationships preventing ambiguity and wasteful impression. Of these an example is the rite of passage by which a youth becomes an adult. Such ritual also helps to integrate the group which takes him on.

Similarly, witchcraft is held by Wilson to support the sociobiological thesis. According to this argument the Shaman, provided that his role is unchallanged, enjoys added power as do his kin. If his actions are not only benevolent but sanctioned through ritual, they contribute to the resolve and integration of society. The biological advantages of institutionalized witchcraft therefore seem clear.

Sanctification also is used by Wilson to confirm his claim, sanctification being defined as the process by which a ritual or belief is certified as unquestionable, death being the punishment for the sceptic. Such sanctification is granted to dogmas and practices in religion that serve the biological interests of the group – to die for God, for king or country. Some modern cults are far from religious but the principle remains. Shintoism, Muslimism, Buddhism and Mao Tse-Tung, Franco and Hitler, all have had people die in their names. 'When the gods are served,' says Wilson, 'the Darwinian fitness of the members of the tribe is the ultimate if unrecognized beneficiary.' Now the question becomes, has the readiness to be indoctrined a genetic basis? Yes is the sociobiological reply (not surprisingly), the fact that blind allegiance can operate in the absence of theology is support enough. Advantage can accrue to both individual and society from such willing subordination. Wilson cites Bergson who argued that without the codification of rules, society would fall apart (and though Wilson does not make it explicit codification depends on indoctrination). However, the arbitrariness of sanctification produces conflict as visionaries and revolutionaries set out to change the system and the stage is set for natural selection at the individual and group levels. These two forms of selection both operate in religious behaviour. Thus group selection favours conformity. Even the loss of genes due to willingness to surrender one's own life is more than balanced by the gain of genes within the surviving group. At the individual level conformity allows individuals to enjoy the benefits of group membership.

I shall stop at this point in the argument because already there are a number of flaws so apparent as to make the whole sociobiological interpretation of religion extremely doubtful. Wilson has criticized many of the popular biologists, such as Ardrey and

Morris as advocates rather than scientists in that they rely on rhetoric rather than scientific evidence and argument. Yet this appears to be true of Wilson's case.

First, note the phrase cultural Darwinism. This phrase has impressive biological connotations suggesting genetic evolution. All it means, however, is that the system that works best tends to survive. For example, if two bus systems operate in town – large buses with conductors and set stops, or small buses stopping anywhere – the two systems will compete until one drops out. This is, in these terms, cultural Darwinism, but it has nothing to do with genes, simply that one suits the traveller better. Thus the statement that the religion which does the practitioners the most good survives adds little to the sociobiological argument unless it is asserted, as it is, that these beliefs have a genetic basis – which is highly unlikely for bus preferences, although a case could be made.

The interactionist argument that religious practices have a genetic basis which is in turn selected for by religious practices seems to me virtually circular or tautologous. Once it is asserted that religious practices have a genetic basis, it follows that the practices that enhance survival will enhance the genes underlying them. In other words, Wilson is saying no more than that religious practices have a genetic basis, which needs evidential support. This support is claimed to be found in ritual. How good are the arguments which I have summarized above?

Before examining these arguments, I should like to point out a good example of Wilson's advocacy. In talking about magic, he likens cave drawings to the intention movements of animals. He cites the waggle dance of the honey bee and writes 'Primitive man would have understood such animal behaviour easily.' I can only ask, how does he know this? Surely this is a wild supposition, that seems to add some kind of biological weight to his claims.

It seems to me no more than assertion that the display of wealth and power in ritualized ceremonies is biologically advantageous to a society. I do not deny that it can be argued, but there is no compelling evidence that this is so. In fact I suspect that the argument turns on a hidden premise which is often found in evolutionary arguments, namely that any behaviour or characteristic must be biologically advantageous and thus selected or else it would not appear. The equally hidden converse argument (which is regarded as convincing) is that behaviour which is not thus advantageous would have disappeared, would have been selected out. This case demands no evidence but it is built into the theory, hence it can be asserted, as here, with some plausibility: military power spectacularly displayed prevents attack by enemies. But this will not do, since it is also part of the evolutionary case that bad characteristics are wiped out and such displays could be in the process of being selected out and in the distant future none might be found. Thus clear evidence of biological advantage is needed. This is especially true when non-biological political and economic reasons for such behaviour can easily be found. Furthermore, characteristics which may not be advantageous, but which are mediated by chromosomes that confer strong biological advantages, may be transmitted by genetic selection for these latter characteristics. Wilson's assertions, plausible though they may be, cannot carry the case.

The argument about witchcraft is again similarly tautologous. The successful Shaman, because he is believed, contributes to the integration and resolve of society and thus its biological advantages are clear. However, it has to be shown, if this argument is not merely that existence proves biological advantage, that shamanism increases resolve and integration more than any other kindred belief system. Wilson nowhere offers any evidence or argument that this is so. The sociobiological claim is, therefore, no more than assertion.

The next point that sanctification of certain values, common to most religions, whether theological or sacred ultimately preserve the Darwinian fitness of the tribe is similarly based upon the evolutionary premise that it must be so. Yet it is necessary to demonstrate that other methods would be less effective. Certainly the Jewish value of non-aggression and attempting to fit with the demands of their host society served them ill in the holocaust. Few Jews would argue that their millions of dead helped to maintain the genes. Nor could it be argued that the fittest survived. Survival was largely fortuitous. Perhaps the very destruction of Jews is seen as ridding the genetic pool of inferior material, as indeed the Nazis believed; but for all its faults, sociobiology is not overtly anti-semitic. In some cases, it is true, heroic self-sacrifice inspired by values has preserved the group, but as I have shown there are counter examples. It seems to me this argument could serve either position –

that self-sacrifice preserved the genes or destroyed them. What is certain is that the claim and its supporting evidence are equivocal.

The final point seems equally dubious, namely that the apparent readiness to be indoctrinated, without which religions (in our broadest sense) would fail, has a genetic basis. Normally to demonstrate a genetic basis biometric methods are used, and similarities in the readiness to be indoctrinated would be shown to occur more in closely related than distantly related individuals, a readiness, furthermore, that could not be attributed to any environmental circumstances. However this is not the approach that Wilson adopts. Instead he cites the philosopher Bergson who argued that codification of rules, based upon indoctrination, keeps society stable. However, this brings visionaries and revolutionaries with radically different ideas into conflict with such rules and thus the stage is set for natural selection. The best man wins and all is best for society. Everything is best in the best of all possible worlds. Once again, we can see that this is no more than the original evolutionary hidden premise, that by definition what is best survives.

I do not want to say more about the sociobiological arguments for the genetic basis of religions. As I have shown, all points are nothing more than plausible assertions. The actual argument is simply that unless religious behaviours preserved genes, they would have died out, but this is the argument that sociobiology is attempting to prove. No real evidence has been produced. This aspect of sociobiology, therefore, is interesting speculation but it is far from being scientifically proven. With detailed study of anthropology and the history of religion, these arguments might be verified but I think that it is difficult to raise them from the level of speculation to verifiable science. This is not necessarily bad in itself, but it runs quite counter to the claims of sociobiology.

Altruism

I will now turn to the question of altruism which, of course, is of central interest to sociobiology since it apparently contradicts its main thesis that an individual's behaviour may be understood as having the aim to perpetuate his genes. Much has been written on this but I will go straight to the horse's mouth and examine what Wilson has to say on this matter.

In his consideration of altruism Wilson suggests the possibility that perhaps conscious altruism is a transcendental human quality that distinguishes human beings from animals, and that this is sufficient explanation. However he is not prepared to take this easy way out. Indeed he claims that it is to the understanding of altruism that sociobiology can make a novel contribution. One argument for not believing altruism to be anything specifically human is that altruistic acts do occur in lower organisms. In the primates and mammals it is occasionally encountered but in the social insects it is relatively common, especially in a form resulting in death, thus making it somewhat comparable to the heroic altruism of man. The biological basis of altruism among social insects is clear; natural selection has been broadened to include kin selection. The deaths of the soldier ants protect the rest of the colony, including more fertile brothers and sisters, and thus the altruistic genes are multiplied by a greater production of nephews and nieces.

The question, therefore, in the case of man's altruism is obvious; can this too be laid at the door of kin selection? The emotion which leads to the great sacrifice could be ultimately genetically selected as the result of favouring relatives over count-less generations, especially when it is remembered that man for most of his history has lived in a social unit consisting of immediate family and a tight network of close relatives. Wilson is forced to concede that the form which altruistic acts actually take is cultur-ally determined: however the emotion which lies behind them has a genetic basis.

Before the evolutionary theory of altruism can be properly appreciated, Wilson argues, it has to be admitted that much of human altruism is self-serving in some sense at least. In many Eastern religions altruism is encouraged but the reward is a better life afterwards, either born again or best of all not born again. Indeed it can be argued that these are not altruistic acts at all but are ultimately selfish. Moreover, the sentiment 'It is a far, far better thing that I do, than I have ever done' may also be ulti-mately selfish, though it may be judged good.

Wilson tries to avoid this difficulty by distinguishing two forms of co-operative behaviour. One he calls 'hard-core' altruism, responses which are relatively unaffected by social rewards or punishments. The impulses are unilaterally directed at others without hope of return. This hard-core altruism is the one operating through kin selection or natural selection working on entire social units. This should serve only the individual's closest kin. Soft-core altruism on the other hand is ultimately selfish. The performer of soft-core altruism expects rewards for himself or his relatives. Such altruism would have evolved by individual selection. Its psychological vehicles are lying, self-deceit, and pretence. Reciprocation is the key to soft-core altruism.

While virtually all altruistic acts among non-humans fall into the category of hard-core, soft-core altruism has been highly elaborated among human beings. Indeed reciprocation underlies the whole structure and edifice of society. However, Wilson argues, it could still be the case that underlying soft is hard-core altruism, the product of our genes. This is highly important because hard-core altruism, programmed genetically, is aimed at the benefit of our relatives. This makes conflict eternal and the likelihood of peace slight.

In brief then, Wilson's argument is that soft-core altruism ultimately aimed at preserving the individual and based upon reciprocation is far better than hard-core altruism. This allows reason to rule the genes, allows for a social contract which, if well engineered on both sides, is probably best for them. Hard-core altruism aimed at the preservation of kin is the basis of ruthless war and conflict. From anthropological studies of immigrants settling into new societies, Wilson argues that, fortunately for civilization, most altruism is soft-core, that is at the crux most individuals work for themselves. He thus takes an optimistic view of the future of society.

I do not intend to say much about these arguments concerning the nature of altruism. They are ingenious but ultimately they descend into matters of speculation rather than clear scientific fact. If it is considered that all actions are ultimately aimed at preserving an individual's genetic material, then soft-core altruism fits the bill. That is, one takes what appears to be altruistic behaviour and presents a plausible case that this is really helpful to preserving the individual genes of those concerned. However this is essentially an untestable assertion. How does one compare the effects of an altruistic solution to a problem to a non-altruistic one? Even a computer simulation of the consequences would not be terribly convincing. Take an example of altruism that is often cited – Mother Theresa who helps the poor of Calcutta, or Schweizer who worked with lepers. This was not hard-core altruism, the heroic act, apparently senseless, ending in glorious death. This is soft-core altruism but serving the preservation of whose genes? Certainly it is possible to argue that both of these have the reward of feeling good, feeling that they are doing a wonderful thing which others cannot bear to contemplate. In this sense it is selfish but it is not gene preservative. Indeed nuns, like Mother Theresa, have vowed not to pass their genes on. How can sociobiology deal with celibacy? Only by calling it hard-core altruism; perhaps, being celibate improves the kin – giving them more opportunity to breed. This, however, reveals the weakness of kin selection as an explanatory concept, because anything that clearly does not favour the preservation of one's genes must favour the preservation of others. Thus any altruistic act can be explained – either it really helps to preserve one's own genes, or it helps to preserve others. It is more simple to see acts as either ultimately preserving one's own genes or preserving others. This is hardly an interesting or important distinction if all acts can be so classified, with no other apparent difference, as in the case of altruism. Once again it appears, regrettably, that the sociobiological analysis of altruism is no more than highly interesting speculation. It provides little understanding of the nature of altruism. This is because, in effect, the concept of kin selection is bound to work, by definition, just as in the case of learning theory once it is agreed that reinforcers produce learning, there is little left to say, a topic which I shall examine in the next section of this chapter.

In conclusion it must be said that sociobiology suffers from the boldness and daring of its approach. It has attempted to deal with fundamental issues of human behaviour and it has produced some brilliant and highly interesting arguments. On analysis, however, it cannot find definitive answers to these questions and it is difficult to see how it ever could do so. Nevertheless, unlike experimental psychology, it has tried and it is to be commended for that.

The work of Skinner

I will now turn to an evaluation, for human psychology, of modern behaviourism. I intend to concentrate upon one of the founders of the whole approach, the definite guru of operant psychology,

B.F. Skinner. He has been a prolific author over the years and I cannot in a chapter of this length deal with all his work. However I will examine some of the most important concepts and ideas in it, a task that is made easier by the recent publication of 'Canonical Papers by B. F. Skinner', in *The Behavioural and Brain Sciences*. Edited by Catania (1985) these are not only key papers to the whole theory but each has a set of commentaries by experts in the field and, even more valuable, replies to these commentaries by Skinner himself.

Before examining this work, I think it is useful to explicate the essence of the behaviourist position. This is so simple that it puts off the casual non-specialist enquirer who feels that it cannot be right (a view with which I heartily concur and which I shall unequivocally demonstrate) but it is this simplicity which has been attractive to scientists, nurtured as they are on Occam's razor (the simplest explanation is best). The Skinnerian position is this: responses which are reinforced tend to recur again, those that are not die away. All behaviour is thus contingent on reinforcement. To understand behaviour, therefore, it is necessary to study the environment to discover what the reinforcers are. There is no need to postulate internal, private, mental events as determinants of behaviour. All such are residues of primitive thinking. Feelings, forces, ideas, spirits, drives, all are quite redundant. From this brief description it is evident that there is a further attraction to scientists especially those who have found in psychology an anodyne to their own inadequacy. It minimizes and denies feelings and emotions. At best they are epiphenomena interfering with a real understanding of behaviour. The psychophobe, as Dixon has called him, has found a philosophy to comfort his agony. To parody the Bard, there is less in heaven and earth than is dreamed of in your philosophy.

One further point remains to be made. The empirical basis of this stems largely from laboratory studies of animals – mainly rats and pigeons. There are considerable inter-species differences in the findings of operant psychology and, furthermore, the type of reinforcer, for example food or water, can affect the results. This is important to bear in mind given the large generalizations which are often made about human behaviour.

There is first a general point about Skinnerian theory which is so obvious and apparently so devastating that it is not usually taken seriously. Certainly when commentators made this point in the canonical papers, Skinner did not consider it worthy of reply. The point is this: if we only do what we have been reinforced to do, then presumably Skinner, also being subject to schedules of reinforcement, writes what he writes simply because he has been so reinforced. There is thus no reason to think that it is true, or more important, that Skinner believes it to be true. Hence why should we bother to examine it? In Skinnerian terms we would be wasting our time, except that if we were examining it, we must have been so reinforced. However, the examination is still quite pointless.

However, I am examining this theory because I do not accept it. Hence it is worth examining so that I can persuade others of its falsity at least as regards its implications for important questions on human behaviour. I see no reason to doubt seriously that lever pressing or pecking in rats and pigeons in a laboratory are quite well understood in operant terms.

Since reinforcement is so central to the work it is important to be clear about its exact meaning. A reinforcer increases the probability of response in an organism. Thus if a pigeon pecks a key and receives food and key pecking increases, food is said to be a reinforcer. If, however, key pecking does not increase, food is not a reinforcer. The point here is that a reinforcer can only be determined by observing its consequences. No common characteristic of reinforcers has ever been found, other than that they reinforce. However, this produces a compete circularity, If we want to explain the increase in frequency of a response, we say, in operant terms, it must have been reinforced. The reinforcer can be spotted because following the response it led to an increase in frequency. This circularity seems to me a serious deficiency in the theory. Unless the nature of a reinforcer can be defined it adds little to our understanding of human behaviour to know that it has been reinforced. I am quite happy to agree that behaviour, to recur, must be reinforced. But as I have argued in my study of the scientific validity of Freudian theory without an operational definition of a reinforcer, we are forced to seek out the nature of reinforcement in the human case and this is precisely what I believe clinical and psychodynamic psychology is really about, if we want to conceptualize it in these terms. Thus it seems quite possible, in human beings, that neurotic behaviour is reinforced because it keeps a horrible feeling or thought at bay out of one's consciousness. This is its reinforcement, even though the more tangible consequences of such behaviour are apparently punishing. Let me illustrate the point, because it demonstrates the feeble explanatory power resulting from the circularity of this definition of reinforcement.

I shall examine agoraphobia, the fear of going out, which is by no means an uncommon presenting symptom in outpatient clinics. What is the reinforcement that keeps this avoidance going? In psychoanalytic theory as described in Fenichel's classic *Psychoanalytic Theory of Neurosis* (1945) it is the fear of being raped. This fear, of course, is a reaction formation to, in the case of a female, her sexual desire which she fears will rage out of control. Thus in terms of reinforcement it is the patient's internal feelings and their assuagement which are the key. This is the human case, immensely more complex than the hooded rat, and one that must ever be beyond the reach of those who study environmental contingencies.

In fact, psychodynamic theory suggests yet another reinforcer may be at work in agoraphobia and in a number of other psychological disorders. This is the masochistic desire for punishment to assuage a guilty super-ego. The punishment in agoraphobia is the considerable nuisance and difficulty which it causes to the patient. In addition it annoys the family and this may be yet a further reinforcer.

I am not claiming that these psychodynamic hypotheses are correct as determinants of agoraphobia, but my point is that such explanations and other mentalistic hypotheses are not inconsonant with learning theory, provided that such mental events are not ruled out of court. It is interesting to note in connection with this point that one of the doyens of behaviour therapy, Rachman no less, has recently (1977) admitted that the simplistic learning theory account of agoraphobia will not do and that research into some of the psychodynamic hypotheses is well worthwhile given the clinical evidence.

Of course if learning theorists had been able to state what the environmental, reinforcing events that maintain phobias and other disorders were (which they are unable to do) recourse to mental events *might* not have been necessary, but note the parenthesis. The reinforcement model (if simply environmental) and the mentalistic model would then represent competing hypotheses, alternatives, and there would be no *a fortiori* necessity to choose the former.

However, the discussion of the circularity of reinforcement and the apparent necessity in the case of agoraphobia to invoke mental events lead to the next point. How are such mental events dealt with in operant psychology? This is examined in a paper by Skinner called 'The Operational Analysis of Psychological Terms', which I will scrutinize in some detail because it reveals, despite its intellectual ingenuity, the fatal weakness of the operant position.

What Skinner is attempting to do is to make genuinely operational the normal subjective language of psychology, for example depressed or cheerful, a task which *prima specie* seems impossible and, in my opinion, is so in fact. Nevertheless, his points must be refuted, if the case is to be dismissed.

It is necessary to know, the argument runs, in the case of most psychological terms, the specific stimulating conditions under which they are emitted and why each response is controlled by its corresponding condition, a question more important than the first. The individual acquires language from society but the reinforcing action of the verbal community continues to play an important role in maintaining the relations between responses and stimuli which are essential to the proper functioning of verbal behaviour. Before continuing with the argument a curious distinction should be noted. Language is said to be acquired from society but reinforced by the verbal community. I am not certain that this is a real distinction, society and the verbal community. It seems equally arguable that language is acquired from *and* reinforced by the verbal community. I fail to see how it could be acquired from any non-verbal group in society. This may be, however, a rather loose use of language.

To understand the conditions responsible for the semantic relation between a verbal response and a stimulus there are three important terms: stimulus, response, and the reinforcement supplied by the verbal community. The community reinforces the response only when it is emitted in the presence of the stimulus which then becomes a discriminative stimulus, an occasion for the emission of the response. This dreadful, convoluted language means simply (what any man in the street or on the notorious omnibus in Clapham would say) that if a child, say, calls a red object red, people understand what he means and respond to him (the reinforcement) and thus he calls other red objects red. If he calls them green or green objects red, there is no such reinforcement (except perhaps among the colour blind) and thus are colours learned. Nothing wonderful so far.

This analysis, Skinner continues, entails that the stimulus acts upon both the speaker and the reinforcing community. If it did not act on the latter it could not reinforce the response. However, and this is the vital point, in *subjective* psychological terms, which are similar to private stimuli, the verbal community cannot reinforce them.

It is, therefore, essential to see how verbal responses to private terms are developed in order to understand how subjective terms are dealt with. In his example of toothache, the speaker reacts to a private stimulus; the verbal community has to infer the stimulus, which is opposed to the scientific hope to be able to predict responses through independent knowledge of the stimulus. How then, does the verbal community, with no access to a private stimulus, generate verbal behaviour in response to it? There are four ways.

1 A child may learn to say 'that hurts' in agreement with the usage of the community, that is reinforcement is contingent upon public accompaniments of painful stimuli – a blow, tissue damage.
2 The response 'toothache' may be elicited by collateral responses to the same stimulus: it is inferred from groans, hands on the jaw, facial expressions – good for malingerers.
3 Some responses to private stimuli are descriptive of the speaker's own behaviour, which when overt forms the basis of the reinforcement by the verbal community. Skinner's example is a person trying to find his way in a dark room.

   If the response is covert it can be regarded as accompanying an overt one which forms the basis of reinforcement or it may be a less intense form (and thus the same) as the overt response. A third possibility is that a response may be emitted to a private stimulus with no public accompaniments. If sometimes, however, there are public manifestations, it can be reinforced.
4 A response to private stimuli may be maintained by public reinforcement through stimulus generalization. Thus internal

states are described as depressed or agitated. These are meta-phors, the response being carried over from the public to the private.

In all these four cases, Skinner argues, the sharpening of refer-ence cannot be achieved by reinforcement by the verbal community as is the case with public events. There is too much room for error in all these categories. Thus a rigorous vocabulary of private events is impossible. Furthermore, there may be distor-tional inaccuracies in the responses, as are fully described in psychoanalysis under the term 'defence'.

These four modes of reinforcement in many cases lead to different meanings being imputed to psychological terms, a point which Skinner exemplifies with hunger. Thus 'I am hungry' can mean 'I have not eaten for a long time' (this is mode 1 in the above analysis), 'my mouth is watering' (mode 2), 'I have hunger pangs' (mode 3). However, although these are synonymous with the words 'I am hungry', they are not themselves synonymous. Whether this matters given their psychological identity is another point. A similar analysis can be made of most commonly used psychological terms. From this Skinner claims that there is no way of basing a response entirely upon the private part of a complex stimuli: 'Differential reinforcement cannot be made contingent upon the property of privacy'.

This objectification of apparently subjective terms such as 'I am hungry' reducing to 'I have not eaten' or 'my mouth is watering', for example, is not entirely convincing, since mouths can water for other reasons than hunger and one is not necessarily hungry even after a long fast. It seems as liable to error as the verbal report itself which indeed can be mistaken. This operationalism is, however, desired by Skinner because it enables a lawful description of the verbal behaviour 'I am hungry' to be made with reference only to public events.

Skinner takes up again the case of red. While red can be objec-tively described as a response to a red stimulus which has been reinforced by the verbal community, there is obviously a difficulty where seeing red becomes a private event, as in the case of imagery – 'I see red' or 'I am conscious of red'. This is explained by arguing that 'I see red' is to react to one's reaction to red. See is a term usually acquired in respect of overt responses available to the community, but it may be evoked by any private accompaniment of overt seeing. Thus private seeing can be slipped in – an example of the third category. Similarly, being conscious can be conceptualized as a form of reacting to one's own behaviour and is thus a social product. Indeed verbal behaviour can be distinguished and defined by the fact that the contingencies of reinforcement are provided by other people (Skinner uses the word 'organisms' but it is relatively so rare that non-humans reinforce that 'people' seems a better word).

As conceptualized here it is difficult to see how language of any complexity could develop. One of Skinner's points is that his account of language must be able to extend to the complexities of his account of language. Now it has been pointed out that in this account it is convincingly shown that language of private events can never be accurate, because essentially it cannot be subject to discriminative reinforcement by the verbal community in contrast to the language of public events. However, the language of science uses terms that are inaccessible and are only loosely tied to stimuli but rather have to be interpreted against a background of theory. Thus theoretical terms will be as crudely reinforced as private terms – hence they should not be used in science! Since Skinner is willing to lower the demands of precision in the scientific case, this can be similarly done in the private case, so the argument falls away. This is a case well made by Danto.

Meehl also has a number of simple points which are essentially fatal to its claims. If I see a red after image it makes good sense for me to describe it as red, referring to my image which is admittedly private. It may be possible to describe it as Skinner does, without recourse to an image, but is this story as convincing – as a reaction to one's reaction to red. Not to me; indeed I see red when I read it. Meehl makes this point with a highly convincing example. The eidetic imager can conjure up an image of a picture with such clarity that he can accurately report details, for example car numbers, number of tiles on a roof and so on. To explain this without invoking an image may be possible but is quite unconvincing. As Meehl argues it is not fatal to a theoretical concept that no one datum compels its inference.

I think all these points render Skinner's attempt to account for private events most unconvincing. There is too a further point. In this explanation, in my view, there is an infinite regress. Just as explanations of mental events in terms of some scanning mechanism imply that within that there must be a scanning mechanism (and thus there is no explanation), so it is in the case of reinforcement by the verbal community. If they were not convinced by their own internal images and sensations, they could not act as reinforcers. In turn their reinforcement has depended upon the convictions of their verbal community. Thus a blind man (and thus it would be if all the verbal community were blinded) cannot give such reinforcement, nor a deaf one to auditory stimuli. All the verbal community does in this approach is to externalize what most psychologists assume is done internally.

Given the implausibility of Skinner's account of internal experiences it is clear that operant psychology is quite unable to deal with the subtlety and complexity of complex human emotions. This alone makes it useless for the programme of research into important human problems such as I drew out in the early chapters of this book. Furthermore, the circularity in the concept of reinforcement, and indeed the difficulty of taking seriously the meaning of a theory which by definition exists only because it has been reinforced by a verbal community, underlines this argument.

Should readers still feel that the evidence for the effects of reinforcers is so clear in animals that it might be wrong to dismiss it in the human case, even if the theory as a whole is inadequate to explain experience, I will cite a recent study by Catania (1986). In this, subjects are reinforced to push a lever in certain directions by the reward of tokens. If during the course of the experiment they are told false rules for operating the lever, despite the reinforcement, they follow the rules. In other words this is a perfect demonstration of why operant conditioning, derived from rats, will not apply in the human case. It can be overruled by language. Thus even in the formal laboratory experiment the Skinnerian model will not do. What is so nice about this experiment is that it shows that external reinforcement does work in the human case but not always, and this latter is the crucial point. If not always, when? We are back at the old clinical problem. In fact probably we know when external reinforcement will work. When verbal rules are hard to formulate or could not be formulated, when therefore man is pushed down nearer to animals, then external reinforcement takes over. This works to some extent with the subnormal.

Enough has been said about operant psychology, formulated so lovingly by Skinner from the laboratory performance of rats and pigeons. Small surprise that it is inadequate for a human psychology. Indeed it is strange that any should ever or still believe it so, although, as I argued earlier in this chapter, its attractions to those who find being human painful are clear enough.

Ethology

I shall now turn to ethology, the study of animals in their natural environment, in contrast to the Skinnerian approach which is strictly laboratory based. Some ethological findings are subsumed under sociobiology, but I want to examine briefly some of the main concepts in ethology to see whether they can be applied to the understanding of human psychology.

Ethology is the study of the behaviour of animals in their natural habitat. It is, therefore, entirely different from the study of the behaviour of animals in the laboratory, the method which was favoured by psychologists until very recently. Ethology has become a branch of biology in its own right and is a huge field. There are two pertinent questions, however, with respect to this book: is it possible to extrapolate from animal to man, and is it possible to conduct useful ethological studies of human behaviour? By ethological, in this later question, I refer not to observational studies but to work which makes use of ethological concepts.

I will deal with the second question first on which so far there is no relevant body of work. My own view is that such research, even if well carried out, would be unlikely to be valuable simply because in his natural habitat man makes considerable use of language. Thus the concepts of ethology, derived from animals, do not seem likely to fit the human case.

This same argument, based upon the importance of language, makes it unlikely that the understanding of animal behaviour derived from ethology would be very powerful in understanding man. Nevertheless, the principles derived from ethology, as distinct from its concepts, could be valuable. For example, if animal aggression were shown to be dependent upon certain releasing environmental stimuli, it might be useful to search for such stimuli in human aggression.

This line of argument has been examined by Hinde (1974), one of the leading British ethologists, and I will now scrutinize his points.

Hinde is quite frank about the problems involved in generalizing from animals to man. Indeed, as he argues, it is dubious enough to generalize from one closely related species to another. Hinde admits that there is an enormous behavioural gap between animals and man – all animals are markedly inferior in their level of cognitive functioning, in their ability to foresee and be aware, and in their ability to reflect on their own behaviour. In the use of language and tools in the development of a complex culture, there is simply no comparison. However, despite these tremendous differences, Hinde argues that comparative studies are valuable because animals are so much more simple. He gives three reasons for this.

First, he claims that the study of animals allows the development of methods which can then be adapted for the human case. He cites the medical sciences as an exemplar: diagnosis and treatment are first worked out with animals and only then applied to man. Some of the techniques and methods used in the diagnosis and treatment of behavioural disorders were also first developed with animals. Furthermore, at a more fundamental level, adequate methods for the description and classification of behaviour were first worked out with animals, and, Hinde argues, such precise description of behaviour is no easy task. He does not claim that descriptions useful for animals are applicable to human behaviour, but rather that they provide a valuable starting point.

I want to make some comments about this first argument. The medical analogy is quite misleading. Medical research tries out, for example, drugs on animals to investigate the effects of large doses. Thus if cancer of the liver develops in mice, it is a possibility that this would occur in man. However, the comparison of precise physiological effects on organs is not like making inferences about the determinants or nature of, say, aggression which are so different in mice and men.

His second point is highly tendentious and somewhat naïve, namely that some of the techniques used in the treatment and diagnosis of behavioural disorders were first developed with animals. The point here is that many psychologists feel that the techniques to which Hinde refers, that is behaviour therapy methods, are grossly unsatisfactory for the vast majority of behavioural disorders precisely because they were developed from animals. Thus there is now agreement that the techniques are not even properly tied to learning theory and that the theoretical rationale is also not consonant with theory, as Rachman has admitted. Furthermore, it is now by no means certain that they are even successful in removing the symptoms. Indeed, it is almost certainly the case that these behavioural methods are best suited to work with grossly subnormal or disturbed individuals, that is individuals whose brain function may, while disturbed, be more close to that of animals. This description is not meant pejoratively but simply descriptively in that, as I have argued in this chapter, it has been shown that conditioning methods do not work with human beings, being overwritten, as it were, by language. Thus this second point does not seem powerful.

Hinde's third point is more general. The relative simplicity of animal behaviour allows precise descriptions to be developed. Thus in the human case it is useful to have such principles of description in mind when trying to make observations. This is true as far as it goes, but it is unfortunately not very far. For example, the neat categories that a hamster's behaviour falls into, grooming, rearing, scrabbling and so on, are hardly useful for the description of human behaviour.

In summary, therefore, Hinde's case is not very powerful. This is by no means to denigrate the contribution of ethology to understanding animal behaviour. All that I am arguing is that on these grounds there is little case for ethology in the study of the critical issues in human psychology. This, however, is only the first of Hinde's arguments and I will now examine his other points.

Hinde's second argument is that for some problems ethical considerations rule out experimentation with human subjects, in which case animals are essential. I will disregard the ethics of animal experimentation (which is a separate issue) but even without this, I fear that this argument is weak, as Hinde's own example shows. He cites the use of monkeys to study the effects of separating infants from their mothers, a subject on which evidence from planned experiments cannot be obtained in man. However, Hinde continues that the findings of such experiments must be generalized to man only with the utmost caution and assessed against more direct sources of evidence. These last two points of caution indicate that really nothing can replace the human evidence. Animal experiments are only sources of sensible hypotheses, certainly not valueless, therefore, but not clearly of critical importance for the study of those psychological topics which I have argued are the true subject matter of psychology.

The third argument which Hinde uses to demonstrate the value of animal work for human psychology is as follows: the study of animal behaviour can provide principles or generalizations whose relevance to man can subsequently be assessed. The examples which Hinde cites are non-verbal communication in animals, the effects of experience on aggressive behaviour in animals and the interaction of mothers and their infants. The animal data are useful here because we can experiment with animals, rear them in controlled conditions and selectively breed them. In these contexts their relevance to man may depend, Hinde argues, on similarities between animals and man 'but they are also rewarding to study just because they are different' (Hinde, 1974).

There are several points here which require comment. Some of his claims are not applicable to ethology which I have defined as the study of animals in their natural habitat. Thus rearing and breeding experiments are ruled out. However, all depends on the similarities between animals and man. Given that generalization to related species is difficult, generalization to man seems impossible. The phrase 'rewarding to study in their own right' is, of course, highly revealing. Again I must point out that I have nothing against studying animal behaviour. All I question is its relevance to an understanding of man. Are principles derived from such work applicable or not? Hinde has some interesting things to say on this point.

Where animals are studied, just because they are different from man, very great care is needed in generalizing the findings to man. Animals are so diverse, Hinde writes, that it is simple to select facts which fit theories and neglect the awkward cases. It is easy, Hinde continues, to bolster up practically any ethical, social or political system. It is also easy to slide from the use of animal metaphors to the implication that they contain something biological and, therefore, basic to human nature. There is a further problem and that is to know at what level of attraction to look for parallels between animals and man. The same principle may find quite different expression in different species and false conclusions may be drawn if comparisons are made at too superficial a level. It is essential to remember, Hinde continues, that it is principles that we are looking for, not superficial similarities in overt behaviour. In addition, such comparisons must not blind us to our specifically human qualities. Indeed the study of animal behaviour can give us perspective on the behaviour of man, for it highlights both what we share with animals and what aspects of us are truly human.

These warnings from one of our most distinguished investigators of animal behaviour are well taken. It is all too easy to seize on evidence from ethology to suit our arguments, ignoring the counter examples. The warning, too, about the sheer diversity of species is vital to remember. All these points make it essential that nothing can be taken from ethology as applying to man until there is clear evidence that this is in fact the case. As with conditioning the essentially human quality, of having language, is the characteristic that may render ethologically derived hypotheses inoperative.

I do not intend to say much more about ethology in the light of the discussion of Hinde's points because I think that its value in the investigation of my definition of what is important in psychology is rather slight.

In the first place none of the concepts used in ethology has ever been shown to be useful in the study of man. Thus in ethology sign stimuli act on innate releasing mechanisms to produce characteristic patterns of behaviour. The red and yellow bill of the herring gull causes the chicks to gape. The round speckled shape of her eggs causes the Golden Plover to sit upon them. Thus a direct contribution from ethology seems to be ruled out.

A second benefit from ethology might be said to be implicit in its nature – that it uses naturalistic, field observation and makes great play with accurate definition of responses and their contextual stimuli. However, although this is certainly valuable in the study of human behaviour the pressure to carry out this type of observation study rather than the artificial methods of the experimental laboratory comes not just from ethology. Thus anthropology is the study of man that is rooted in and centred upon field observations and, as I have shown in earlier chapters, the scientific method itself demands accurate observation. Indeed, a combination of rigorous science and anthropology should effectively yield a human ethology. In brief, my argument is that ethology has contributed little to the understanding of human behaviour.

However, there is a more fundamental point which, in the end, must mean that ethological studies are essentially irrelevant to the human case. This is most clearly seen in aggression. Now there seems to be one important common element in human aggression through the ages. This is that, in general, aggression, certainly of the more destructive kind, is between groups, and is sustained by often fanatical belief in the virtues of the group. Nationalism, religious fervour, political belief, these three notions alone have been cruelly destructive.

Now consider what ethologists have to say concerning the causes of aggression in animals. I summarize Hinde's excellent study of *Biological Bases of Human Social Behaviour* (1974) for this purpose. Proximity is a factor in animal aggression. The more crowded the situation the more likely is aggression to be elicited, although even here there are exceptions, as in the hamadryad baboon. The internal state of the individual affects his aggression – endocrine state, which varies through the seasons, is important. Sometimes testosterone, the male hormone, increases aggressive behaviour either directly or indirectly as in the red deer, where antler size is the eliciting stimulus. Sometimes it is 'nervous states' as in the great tit where feeding is interspersed with aggression. There are many other such elicitory factors in aggression discussed by Hinde, all of a similar sort.

In the context of human aggression, this kind of observation really does appear to be irrelevant. Thus the ancient Greeks attacked and killed non-Greeks as if they were animals. The term Barbarian was used by them for such non-human groups. The Inquisition saw the slaughter of deviant heretics from orthodox Christianity. Later witches were burned. In more modern times, Jews and inferior groups were killed by pure Aryans (in fact a mythical category), Republicans kill Loyalists in Ireland (or Catholics Protestants), on the borders of Iran and Iraq two sects of Muslims have been slaughtering one another for five years without sign of cessation, and all Muslims are dedicated to the destruction of non-Muslims. To understand this needs all the resources of psychoanalysis (learning theory looks unimpressive here) and social psychology has to rely on the concept of the out-group (but whence the group?).

Not all the intricate study of wood wasps and ants, or colonies of hamadryad baboons and chimpanzees or shoals of white whales and dolphins or horseshoe bats, upside down in their twilight caves, can bear on this phenomenon. Alas, despite the precision and the attraction of its observations, ethology will not do the trick.

Some have argued that, even if in the case of aggression ethology has failed, nevertheless some minor victories must be acknowledged. Imprinting might be cited as an example of this. Imprinting refers to the rapid learning of a response at a time when the animal is particularly ready to do so. Thus, when hatched from the eggs, young fowl tend to follow the first moving object which they see. Lorenz has had many a goose imprint his image. Of course imprinting, as such, has never been shown to occur in man. Nevertheless, there do seem to be critical periods for learning certain important things. Language learning, for example, probably is subject to a critical period, and if not learned by six years, it becomes very much more laborious, judging from the evidence of feral children (and assuming that these are not autistic).

However, critical periods for learning are far more general than the notion of imprinting, and such a concept as the critical period is not really dependent upon any ethological observation even though ethological studies may have helped to stimulate interest in them. However, such stimulation could not support ethological study on its own. Nothing that ethology has found can contravert the claim that the proper study of man is man not animals. Certainly the nature of human aggression, as I have shown, makes it clear that the ethology of animals is irrelevant.

Professor Dixon of University College London, whose encouragement has helped me greatly in the completion of this book, but who cannot be blamed for any of its defects, has suggested that here I have been too severe on ethology. He argues for example that in matters of sexual attraction, ethological notions may well be useful. His is a view put strongly by Morris, who cites the shape of women's buttocks and breasts as being sign stimuli for male sexual responses.

There are two points here. First, if these are sign stimuli it is curious how tastes change over time and differ between cultures. The well-rounded curves of Botticelli and Rubens, for example, would cut little ice with the modern male persuaded by advertising and fashion that the skeletal and gaunt frames of anorexia are sexually attractive. However, even if breasts and buttocks are sign stimuli this is nothing more than a descriptive label. Human beings appear to have been well aware of their sexual attractions since the time of literacy. Ethology has certainly added no new knowledge on this point.

I have one final objection to this ethological viewpoint in the matter of sexual attraction, let alone love. Cultural factors are enormously influential, such as the jobs people do, their reputations, in some cases their marital status, their families. This was well summed up by Jacqueline Kennedy when discussing her love for Onassis: she said she found money sexually exciting. Such symbolic fetishism is only possible in man. It is factors such as these and the fact that in these instances the notion of sign stimuli is purely labelling that leads me to differ from Dixon on this point.

Conclusions

My final conclusion to this chapter can be brief. My scrutiny of three important branches of the study of animal behaviour has shown them all to be wanting in the study of man. The Skinnerian approach just does not fit the behaviour of human beings, as the experimental studies of Catania indicate. Furthermore, the absurd straitjacket approach of reducing the complex mental world of human beings to overt or covert responses, even if possible, yields nothing valuable.

Sociobiology was shown to be highly interesting but at the present state of knowledge, little more than speculation based upon dubious generalization from animals to man. Preserving one's genes or those of one's kin does not seem sufficient to account for all we do.

Finally, ethology was shown, too, to be insufficient to illuminate human behaviour. As with operant conditioning and sociobiology, the enormous distinction between man and animals (ultimately I presume, attributable to his cortex), confirmed by the use of language and the complexity of its concomitant culture, renders ethology weak for the study of human behaviour. In sum, man is an animal but is a unique animal and thus he needs to be studied in his own right.

Chapter eight

A way ahead

So far in this book I have found little to say which is good about experimental psychology. Yet I do not intend to do a demolition job, to put the boot in, to provide a final solution for experimental psychology.

So that my constructive proposals which constitute this final chapter can be properly evaluated, I will first set out the points that I have made so far in this scrutiny of experimental psychology. I consider that the following propositions have been irrevocably established.

1 Experimental psychology studies trivial topics which are divorced from what most people believe to be important in their lives.
2 This is largely due to the reliance of experimental psychology on 'the scientific method'.
3 This method was shown to be, as conceived in psychology, unsuited to most important problems in psychology.
4 Despite its failure to produce results, the scientific method was grimly adhered to in experimental psychology for a number of reasons.
   (a) the high prestige of science in the *Zeitgeist*;
   (b) the concentration of experimental psychology in universities where science and pure research were prestigious and better funded than the arts;
   (c) the emphasis in scientific experimental psychology on intellect rather than feeling is reinforced by the Western educational system which ignores the latter, concentrating almost entirely on intellect;

(d) promotion in universities depends upon the numbers of publications; adherence to the scientific method allows rapid publication on currently fashionable topics;

(e) individuals who are afraid of their emotions and feelings are attracted into scientific psychology, hence the failure to deal with these important topics.

5 Despite this clear disjunction between experimental psychology and what might be called 'real' psychology, it could be the case that experimental psychology had discovered important things.

6 Scrutiny of various subject areas of psychology showed, unfortunately, that this was not the case. Topics held by leading specialists in the relevant fields to be vital and important, turned out to be little more than detailed description with no implications for broad theory or application.

7 Indeed in this sense it can be argued that experimental psychology resembles hermeneutics rather more than science.

8 Hence the subtitle 'The Emperor's New Clothes', referring to the whole edifice of experimental psychology. To the naïve observer, experimental psychology looks totally worthless. Remove the trappings of science and academe and it is.

However, nakedness has to be covered. The purpose of this chapter is to suggest ways in which psychology can progress, can tackle what are clearly truly important issues in human life and can become as it should be, a truly vital subject. For most people, it must be kept in mind, their own condition, their own feelings are the real interest of their lives. Thus psychology should be the most popular subject of all. If people go to sleep in seminars and lectures (given that this is not a defence) then there is something seriously wrong. In my experience of these events, on this criterion there is indeed trouble. Most psychology is more powerful than Mogadon.

I am not so arrogant as to discuss methods of psychological investigation so arcane and ingenious as to be beyond the grasp of other research psychologists. No indeed, this final chapter is more modest than that. Instead I want to discuss some approaches that do seem to overcome many of the problems and difficulties which have already been discussed. The fact is, and it is hardly surprising, that some researchers have hit upon methods that can deal with the unconscious and its emotional conflicts, and some have not eschewed the unconscious through fear of emotion.

Percept-genetics

I now want to discuss percept-genetics, an approach to the investigation of the unconscious and its emotional conflicts which does seem to overcome many of the limitations of more traditional experimental psychology. Percept-genetics is a theoretical approach to perception as it influences behaviour, together with a set of measurement techniques, developed in Scandinavia by Kragh and Smith (1970).

It studies the development of perception usually by investigating subjects' reports of stimuli presented subliminally and tachistoscopically in a series at gradually decreasing speeds. For example, a stimulus will be shown very rapidly and a description of it obtained from a subject. At the next exposure in the series, a little less rapidly, another (more full) report is obtained until by the end of the series, a veridical or nearly veridical description can be given.

In percept-genetics, following the Gestalt tradition, perception is conceptualized as a process between the individual and the stimulus. This constructive process, normally in the real world instantaneous and beyond introspection, can be examined by 'fragmenting' the stimulus in the tachistoscopic series of presentations. The serial presentation effectively prolongs and makes visible a normally automatic process. For example if in real life we see an apple, our perception of the apple depends not only on the retinal stimulation provided by the fact but on all our previous knowledge and experience of apples. Hence the difficulties that the blind experience on restoration of sight. It is this cognitive and affective aspect of perception that percept-genetic methods seek to uncover.

Kragh and Smith in their collection of papers try to demonstrate that the percept-genetic methods allow observation of the events and life experiences crucial to the emotional development of the individual and the unconscious mechanisms and associated drives habitual to the individual.

Various stimuli could be used to reveal this information but one set, the Defence Mechanism Test (DMT) (Kragh, 1969), is most widely used. These stimuli consist of two pictures differing in detail. Each has three elements: a central figure, the hero, with which subjects are supposed to identify, the hero's attribute (gun, car or violin) and a threat figure, a man or woman with a hideous threatening face. Parallel sets of cards with male and female figures for the two series are used. In fact these stimuli are adaptations from Murray's Thematic Apperception Test (TAT).

Reports, that is drawings and descriptions, of the stimuli as they are presented at gradually decreasing speed are obtained and scored for the presence or absence of defence mechanisms, the unconscious distortions with which we view the world. An objective scoring scheme with high reliability has been developed for the materials by Kragh and Smith.

Validity of the DMT as a measure of defence

Sjoback (1967), Westerlundh (1967) and Kragh and Smith (1970) discuss many clinical studies using the DMT. Essentially it can be said that the technique can discriminate clinical groups and that, in some cases at least, highly interesting material about personal and previously forgotten events was uncovered. Concerning the DMT as a measure of defence mechanisms all that is offered is face validity: thus in scoring a protocol for denial, a process similar to that described by Freud is scored. An example will illustrate this point. If at exposure number three a subject writes 'I think I can see a face in the corner of the picture' but at exposure four continues 'No, it is not a face, it is a vase curved and sloped', then denial would be scored. Recently, however, in Exeter, we have carried out studies of percept-genetics which go further to confirm the claim that defence mechanisms can be measured by these techniques.

The first study (Kline and Cooper, 1977) was a pilot investigation aimed to see whether, by using different methods, even more clear defence mechanisms could be observed. For this purpose we used a card which shows a pig suckling and a neutral control card of a pig from an advertisement for Harris bacon. Eight subjects were administered the two cards using the percept-genetic methods.

Examination of the protocols was convincing. To the suckling pig, expected to elicit defences against oral erotism, there were typical defensive distortions. For example, a denial of a picture of a pig feeding; or complete failure to see any animals at all. To the bacon advertisement there was nothing of this sort.

Further, Cooper and Kline (1986) carried out an intensive study of the DMT in which the scores were related to other personality variables and to the perceptual defence measures of repression. We found that the general factor in the DMT correlated with the difference in threshold of recognition for the words, VD and TV. Such threshold differences are virtually operational definitions of Freudian repression. In addition this factor was able to predict success in pilot training: the correlation was .49.

We regard this finding as support for the validity of the DMT as a measure of defences on the following grounds. Defences are used to ward off threat. In high-speed jet flying there is a variety of threats, in combat rather than civil aviation, especially in low-level sub-radar defence screen operations. Those whose reaction to threat is defensive are less likely on purely theoretical grounds to be as efficient as those whose responses are reality based. This was the rationale used by Kragh (1969) for the use of this test in the Swedish Air Force, where it was successful as it has been in other forces. In my view this work, along with the Swedish clinical work, suggests that percept-genetic methods are useful in the study of the unconscious.

Next I want to discuss the work of Silverman (1983), work which resembles, to some extent, percept-genetics, which, as we have seen, offers some promise for investigating the unconscious. Silverman's approach is known as the Drive Activation Method. In this stimuli which are thought to be, in psychoanalytic theory, drive or conflict activating are presented subliminally to subjects. Similarly it is possible to present drive reducing stimuli. Measurements of psychological disturbance are taken before and after the presentation of these stimuli so that it is possible to gauge the effects produced. The rationale of the method is straightforward and is rooted in basic psychoanalytic theory which, in consequence, is put to a severe empirical test. In psychoanalytic theory psychological disturbance or psychopathology is held to be caused by unconscious conflict. Hence if the conflict can be aroused or reduced there should be changes in symptomatology. Furthermore, it should be noted that if the conflict is made conscious there ought to be no effect at all, since the conflict which produces the psychopathology is unconscious. This last point provides a good basis for experimental control since the same stimuli presented above the recognition threshold should have no effects on psychopathology. Thus the whole experimental design with all the requisite controls is really capable of investigating what, if any, unconscious conflicts are related to psychopathology. The typical experimental design is set out below and the neat logic becomes obvious.

A conflicting stimulus is presented subliminally and above the threshold of recognition.

A neutral stimulus is thus twice presented.

A drive-reducing stimulus is thus twice presented.

With the drive-arousing stimulus psychopathology should be increased in the subliminal case. With the drive-reducing stimulus psychopathology should be decreased in the subliminal case. With all other presentations there should be no effects. In other words what is important in this experimental design is the total pattern of results. It has to be said that in more than eighty experiments carried out by Silverman and his colleagues and students, such a pattern of results has been exhibited, almost without exception.

Further subtleties can be introduced into these experiments. For example, in psychoanalytic theory, stutterers are said to be fixated at the anal level of development. This means that anal matters are likely to be a source of unconscious conflict. Schizophrenics, on the other hand, are fixated at the oral level so that things oral are critical here. Thus if oral and anal stimuli are used with schizophrenic and stuttering subjects, it is possible to hypothesize which individuals will be upset by some stimuli and which by others. As was the case with the pattern of results such differential effectiveness has been discovered.

Some authors have attempted to argue that a better control than the neutral stimulus would be a stimulus that is generally and openly unpleasant. However, such stimuli, however presented, do not produce increases in psychopathology. Furthermore, the differential findings where specific stimuli are given to specific subjects as was the case with stutterers and schizophrenics effectively answers this criticism. Before commenting upon the value of this work I will briefly describe some of the stimuli and the measures of psychopathology because these aspects are open to criticism.

Stimuli include a snarling man with a dagger in his upraised hand; a growling tiger chasing a monkey; a roaring lion; a man with bared teeth attacking a woman. Sometimes there are verbal stimuli, such as Mummy and I are one; my girl friend and I are one (to investigate symbiosis); beating Dad is wrong or beating Dad is okay.

The measures of psychopathology are undoubtedly the weakest aspect of Silverman's Drive Activation Method. These consist of rating scales (for sexual arousal, for example), word association measures, or indices from the Rorschach test. Unfortunately, none of these measures is renowned for its validity and particular caution must always be shown with the Rorschach:interpretation of inkblots is notoriously unreliable.

Despite these caveats I think the Silverman method deserves further research and is a most promising device for the investigation of unconscious material and its influence on our conscious awareness for the following reasons, even though I am cautious in my evaluation of all the work which has been so far completed. First, I think that it is essential that the work be replicated by researchers who are entirely independent of Silverman and his colleagues. This is not because I think that there is cheating or dishonesty of any kind, but it is always possible that, in the work of one laboratory, there is a specific artefact affecting the results. Some independent work is now being done and in one study of the effects of damping down oedipal conflicts (beating Dad is okay) in learning statistics, the findings were in accord with psychoanalytic hypotheses. In other words oedipal conflicts are implicated in the well-known difficulties that most people have in learning mathematics. Such independent replication is clearly essential.

There is no doubt, too, that the measurements of psychopathology are weak, as I have indicated. However, these can quite easily be improved and the fact that a pattern of results emerges, which is in accord with psychoanalytic hypotheses but which is difficult to explain with any other hypotheses, suggests that the rating scales were not so poor as to render results meaningless. In brief, this problem of the measurement of psychopathology is by no means insurmountable.

137

The stimuli used by Silverman reflect his particular interests in psychoanalytic theory. However, any conflict-laden stimulus could be chosen. One of the most effective methods of investigating the unconscious would be to tailor subliminal stimuli to individuals' conflicts. Thus if we knew from free associations and dream material that an individual has a particular unconscious conflict, a stimulus could be designed to tap it, thus comprehensively testing both psychoanalytic theory and the Silverman experimental method. In addition to this, the method allows any normally unconscious material to be shown subliminally. Thus the unconscious would be openly examined, and its nature in relation to psychopathology could be laid bare for all to see and the claims of all analysts could be compared.

Because of the problems with the method which I have fully examined, I do not intend to discuss any of the findings in this book. What I think has been shown so far by the Silverman method is that it offers opportunities to study the role of the unconscious in psychopathology. This means that it is a method which fits the picture of what I have argued is important in psychology and what truly merits investigation.

As was pointed out by Dixon (1971) there has been strong resistance from experimental cognitive psychologists to psychodynamic interpretations of subliminal perception studies of any kind. The original perceptual defence work which showed that thresholds to threatening and to neutral words were different was always explained away as experimental artefact, some unwanted demand characteristic of the experimental procedure until Dixon himself devised a method which was not open to such attacks.

I mention this point because, as I have implied in my discussion of Silverman's drive activation technique, this method and the consequent interpretation of the findings are not accepted by most experimental psychologists. There is a further important issue of direct relevance to the acceptability of the results. This is the relation of the Silverman method to the percept-genetic techniques. If a clear and sensible relationship between the two approaches could be demonstrated, most of the experimental objections would be *ipso facto* answered.

As I write this Westerlundh (1976), who has taken up the percept-genetic mantle in Lund, has reported research which bears simultaneously upon both these projects. Although this is highly specialized work, I think that the results are so important, answering many objections both to percept-genetics and to Silverman's Drive Activation Method, that I must discuss this research. His results certainly support my contention that both these methods are capable of dealing with emotions and unconscious conflicts.

Spence, a cognitive experimental psychologist, has argued that Silverman's interpretation of his work, which, as we have seen, involves subjects processing the subliminal stimuli, must be wrong because, essentially, such processing of subliminal stimuli is impossible. He argues that any results, which are almost impossible to replicate, can be explained away by what is known about perceptual processing: in effect Silverman's results are artefacts of his experimental technique. Spence is quite specific, pointing to three components of the experimental set-up: the place in the visual field where the message is presented, its visual angle and the number of lines in the message. Spence finds, unlike Silverman, that peripherally presented words are not processed, that it is not likely that messages presented on more than one line can be read as a whole and that location in the visual field is a vital determinant of the outcome: only short-time messages presented so that they are first processed by the left hemisphere are interpreted syntactically. If they are presented so that they are first processed by the right hemisphere, an often idiosyncratic interpretation of individual words prevails. Such artefactual, method related factors Spence uses to reinterpret Silverman's findings which, Spence claims, are difficult to replicate. The interpretation favoured by Spence rejects psychodynamic hypotheses of a dynamic unconscious, and proposes instead a content free unconscious system working on probabilistic rather than psychodynamic principles.

As I argued in my discussion of Silverman's findings, such a cognitive interpretation is not favoured by the psychoanalytically meaningful pattern of results with differential stimuli for example, that have been found by Silverman. Nevertheless, given the problems of replication, Spence's objections need to be answered. The work by Westerlundh does this entirely effectively.

First, Westerlundh showed that drives could be activated as claimed by Silverman. However, the verbal stimuli were not shown through a tachistoscope but were left exposed at a subliminal level of illumination for seven seconds, thus allowing processing, and overcoming Spence's objections to the tachisto-scopic method. The measurement of psychopathology was percept-genetic defences as measured by the Defence Mechanism Test which I have described.

What was important about the results was that there were acti-vation effects even when the subliminal stimuli were nonsensical. Thus in the depression condition the following statements were equally potent in activating defences: 'Mummy is worthless', 'I am worthless' and 'the bleak is worthless'. ('Bleak' is a Swedish word for a kind of fish.) What this indicates, as Westerlundh points out, is that in the subliminal reading of words, there is a special process: negatively toned parts (worthless) increase acti-vation of anxiety and defences, while positively toned parts reduce this. Thus there is probably a simple hedonic calculus. Neutral words are disregarded and positive and negative words combine in a global, holistic way to give a total emotional meaning.

Given this type of unconscious analysis there are considerable limitations as to the verbal stimuli which can be used in the Drive Activation Method. Thus 'Mummy is killing me' is not probably as threatening as 'this shoe is killing me' because Mummy is positively toned. Although these findings apply particularly to the method of subliminal presentation used by Westerlundh, he argues convincingly that these same strictures apply to Silverman's method of subliminal presentation especially when the verbal stimuli are long or on many lines. Thus Spence is correct when he argues that normal syntactic processing is impossible, but an hedonic calculus can be used.

In brief, Westerlundh's work confirms that Silverman's Drive Activation Method is viable even allowing for some of the objec-tions of the experimental cognitive psychologists. It links the method well with the percept-genetic approach which almost certainly provides a good method of measuring the effects of the drive activation model. In addition it suggests that the construction of activating or calming stimuli should be in terms not of seman-tics, but of total hedonic tone of the words used. This work certainly confirms the value both of percept-genetic methods and of Silverman's drive activation techniques in the study of emotional and unconscious mental processes.

One point now remains unsettled. This is the difficulty in replication which has been reported from other laboratories. To some extent, however, Westerlundh's findings explain these. Much depends upon the length of verbal stimulus, where it was within the total picture, matters on which Silverman was not always explicit. This means that in some experiments only part of the stimuli may have been processed, thus altering the total hedonic value and the results. With this explanation, I think it is possible to argue that Silverman's method is viable for the investigation of unconscious mental activity.

There is a third approach which I have tried out in a number of researches and which could be valuable if well executed. This is the G analysis of projective tests. G analysis, which I do not intend to describe in detail, is a method of factor analysing objectively scored projective tests. My reasons for thinking this *might* – and I emphasize here that this is a highly speculative method – prove useful are as follows.

Even the most avowed enemies of projective tests admit that it is possible that they tap some hidden or unconscious material in their subjects. The main problem is how can this be interpreted properly, that is how valid are such measures? This general lack of evidence for the validity of projective tests is compounded by their low reliability. As a result many scientific psychologists have abandoned them.

G analysis involved scoring the response to the projective test for the presence (1) or absence (0) of any characteristic. These 1s and 0s are then factored, on their own or with other tests. An example will clarify the point and enable us to see the value of G analysis in the research use of projective tests. In the House Tree Person Test, in which, as the name suggests subjects have to draw a house, a tree and a person, there are many surprising interpretations. For example if no path is drawn to the front door, this is held to be defensive. The subject wants to hide away and not be known. The age of the tree is said to reflect the emotional maturity of the subject. If all these claims were true, of course, projective tests would be highly valuable in the type of psychology I have advocated.

Suppose that Subject 1 had drawn a house without chimneys and a huge front door. In G analysis no chimney and a huge front door would be variables. Subject 1 would score one for each of these. Suppose Subject 2 drew a house of corrugated iron with a broken window. A broken window would be a variable as would the corrugated iron house. Subject 2 would score one for each of these but nil on the previous variables. In this way projective test responses can be reliably scored and factoring could show some highly interesting points.

Again an example will clarify this point. In the Manual to the House Tree Person Test, it is claimed that a subject who described his tree as a soft maple tree was showing unconscious fears of impotence! Now the response 'maple' to a drawing of a tree is quite sensible on the conscious level. Thus in a factor analysis 'soft maple' would be expected to load on two factors: (1) a conscious ego factor, and (2) an unconscious factor or even a castration fear factor. If, therefore, in the factor analysis we had clear indicators of unconscious measures, for example a repression measure which was mentioned in the discussion of percept-genetics, it would be possible to tease out the unconscious implications, if any, of projective tests and thus gain good insights into those areas of emotion and conflict which are so important in the lives of most of us. As I have said, I cannot claim that such a procedure would yield the information we seek, but I think that there is a strong possibility, far stronger than is the case with standard experimental methods.

I have now described three methods in psychology which I think can be useful in dealing with what I have argued are the most important and humanly salient problems in psychology. I am not claiming that these are the only methods or even that they are the best methods. Rather I put them forward to show that even now, although it has reached a low ebb, experimental psychology can go some way to investigating unconscious and conflict laden minds.

However, these methods, it has to be frankly admitted, are limited; there are many aspects of psychology to which they are not particularly well suited. That is why in the final part of this book, I sketch in an outline of an education for the kind of psychology which I hope to see. For in this educational plan there will be emphasis on innovation and creativity, on attempting to produce new and unknown methods and approaches rather than on the reproduction of what is already known.

Before I turn to these educational innovations, however, I want to discuss briefly an aspect of experimental psychology to which many psychologists object, objections which have been implicit rather than explicit in my analysis of the problems of experimental psychology. These objections deserve to be made quite explicit because they are probably as important in contributing to the failure of experimental psychology to deal adequately with topics salient to the human condition, as the more obvious difficulties I have already discussed. These implicit objections are really concerned with values and attitudes – attitudes to human beings and how they should be treated, attitudes which are, of course, rooted in the values of the psychologist. For this part of my book, I am indebted to Dr Penny Pickering for discussions on the nature of psychology.

Human values in psychology

In my study of the scientific method as applied in psychology, I have showed how methods that work well in the natural sciences seem inadequate when applied to the human case. Cattell (1981), indeed, had argued that we study personality as we might investigate the mechanism of a watch. The emphasis on the scientific method was on objectivity, quantification, the negation of human judgement. In fact, much of modern experimental psychology is bound to computers, not just for the analysis of data, but for the presentation of stimuli and the recording and measurement of responses, as well as the final statistical analysis. In addition, computer models and simulations are common-place in experimental psychology.

Now as the comparison of human personality (a most subtle and almost ineffable concept in literature) to a watch indicates, experimental psychology regards human beings as objects or, at best, mechanisms. Many people with humane values consider that treating human beings as objects is unpleasant and unacceptable. On these grounds alone academic psychology, for them, can be entirely rejected – almost regardless of what might have been discovered. I shall explore this objection further.

As soon as people are regarded as objects their value is diminished. This ultimately is why democracy is a more civilized form of government than any other because each person is equally valued because he or she is a person and not for any other reason. In many other forms of government classes of people, those not in the government elite, are seen as objects for the use of the state. Thus in capitalist societies people are seen as objects for increasing wealth and producing goods (for this reason they are replaced by other more efficient objects – robots and computers) and they are now considered useless, fit only for mounting bicycles to more distant places yet to see a robot. In communist countries people are regarded essentially as objects serving the interests of the state. As in slave societies of the past, such objects are kept by the state in as good condition as is possible so that the production of wealth may continue. In Nazi Germany the treatment of people as objects is seen at its most extreme and is thus particularly revealing. Jews and Poles were regarded as objects whose function was to produce. They were not fed, thus keeping down costs, wore out after six weeks and were replaced. Beautiful young Aryan girls were mothers, reproducers of the super race. Slavs and Russians were to be slaves. National Socialism was the objectification of man, man as a machine, taken to its most vicious extreme. The experimental method as applied to man is part of that same fascistic orientation. As such it is deplored by those who value human beings for being human. It is, of course, a terrible irony that the objects of experimental psychology are invariably called subjects. Such a use of words, the equivalence of opposites, has been well documented by Freud and in more deliberate vein by Orwell in *1984*.

However, such gross and vicious treatment of people as objects, in its extreme and most violent form in Nazi Germany, and endemic now in Thatcherite Britain, but in a guise less overtly cruel, is not the sole consequence of the objectification of individuals. Objectification permeates every aspect of life and none so more significantly than education and medicine in their widest sense.

Thus if we take education: in an objectifying and mechanistic society, children are regarded as empty vessels to be filled with the knowledge that society sees fit for them to have. In such a society and with such a view of man, the teacher is an authority figure, the font of wisdom. This is teaching by fiat. There is little participation in education by the taught, they are the receptacles of knowledge. This inert and dehumanizing process is, of course, a bulwark to change, a recipe for a status quo in which objects do and move as they are told.

In such a system, where teachers know and have authority, it is hardly surprising that we find an emphasis on factual knowledge and difficult and complex techniques and methods all of which have to be rigorously acquired by the novitiate. Hence the emphasis in experimental psychology on mathematics and statistics, on qualifications and examinations, and in the universities the awesome hierarchy of the professoriate and their degrees all marked by gowns of illustrious weave and tone. The scarlet robes of doctors grace the antique walls of Oxbridge and make a banquet splendid. Thus in authoritarian society is learning defined, but who now cares what Plato wore as he addressed his students? In a society where people are valued as human beings the form of education is very different and this must be kept in mind when my proposals for a new education in psychology are discussed below.

However, there is a further ramification of objectification which is perhaps even more germane to my thesis and this in the field of medicine and psychiatry, and in the latter good psychology would be expected to play an important part. I do not want here, and certainly do not have the space, to go deeply into the nature of psychosomatic medicine and the psychological aspects of many organic disorders including cancers and diseases of the heart. However, there can now be no doubt that psychological factors are implicated in most diseases. However, the objectivity of science to which the profession and education of doctors is wedded (far more firmly indeed than is psychology) means that treatment is generally in the experimental tradition. A patient presents and the work of the doctor is to diagnose the malfunction in the object and treat it by drugs or by surgery. Lip service may be paid to the psychological factors, but to paraphrase a comment, actually of a psychiatrist, the only time a patient should open his mouth is to receive his pills. However, the fact that physicians, deluded by science, treat their patients as objects is secondary (*vis-à-vis* my thesis) to the implications for psychiatry and the treatment of psychological disorders.

When people come to either psychiatrists or psychologists for help because they are in distress it is not uncommon for them to be diagnosed depressive, schizophrenic, manic, neurotic, anxious, agoraphobic, anorexic and given some appropriate treatment. This is very much a medical model of mental disturbance. It assumes that there is something wrong with the mechanism and if this error can be precisely located, it can be remedied. This mechanistic approach to mental disturbance, aesthetics aside, is not highly successful. Millions of pills a day are absorbed into millions of bloodstreams in the hope that some better feelings will ensue. In most cases all in vain. The deteriorated schizophrenic is still a common sight.

. Suppose, however, that people are not treated as objects that have gone wrong but are sympathetically listened to as individuals worthy of respect whose disturbed feelings and emotions reflect unhappy events and experiences. In this case they would not be labelled as psychiatrically ill and given drugs or other even more stringent interventions, such as electric shock treatment, but rather they would be given psychotherapy so that they could come to see their problems in a new light and possibly accept them or feel, as a result, strong enough to make changes in their lives. Psychotherapy, based upon respect for the person, then puts psychiatric illness and disturbance into an entirely new light. This is the difference between the humane view and the scientific objective view of man. I am not claiming, of course, that such psychotherapy will always be successful but that in some cases it will relieve suffering. As Freud said, 'What we can hope for from psychoanalysis is to replace neurotic misery with ordinary, everyday unhappiness.' The same applies to psychotherapy whether psychoanalytic or not.

I want to exemplify my point by briefly examining depression. I am sure we all have experienced depression from time to time. Clinical depression is a more intense and chronic form of this most unpleasant experience. In a well-known study of Camberwell housewives, Brown and his colleagues showed that about 30 per cent of a large sample were effectively clinically depressed (Brown and Harris 1978). They also demonstrated that significant factors in this depression were having two or more young children, a partner in whom it was difficult to confide and a mother who died in childhood.

If such women turn up for treatment of their depression it is highly likely that they will be labelled, as was done by Brown, depressive, and given a regular dose of anti-depressants, or Valium or its Health Service equivalent. However, as Smail has eloquently argued in *Illusion and Reality* (1984) is not this objectified treatment a monstrous insult? What in the lives of these women should prevent them from being depressed? It is, in fact, a commentary on our society that mothers are so treated that they are enclosed with their offspring without companionship or anything that is likely to make them feel happy.

Thus the objectification of people, the basis of the scientific approach to psychological and psychiatric disorders, as exemplified by depression, is in fact a political act. It supports the status quo. It assumes that all is well in society and that if women feel depressed there is something wrong with them. Listen to them, on the other hand, and we can discover that perhaps there is something wrong with society.

Of course, I am not arguing that psychotherapy based upon respect for individuals can cure these ills. However, it may lead these women to review their problems and take the appropriate action. Thus psychotherapy and its obverse, the objectification of individuals, are essentially political acts – the former radical, the latter conservative. Small wonder that psychotherapy meets with such opposition.

At this point I want to consider, briefly, the anomalous instance of behaviour therapy. The essence of behaviour therapy is that psychological problems are conceptualized as learned responses or behaviours which are inappropriate. The treatment, therefore, consists of replacing the inappropriate responses with more fitting responses. Such treatment leans heavily on learning theory and conditioning. This is raised here because such therapy is truly treating the individual as object. Learning theorists write always of predicting and controlling behaviour and behaviour therapy instantiates this claim. It presupposes that the therapist knows what behaviour is right and correct. It is a supreme example of man the controller. Even as little boys play with electric trains, so do behaviour therapists control their patients. It is even more unpleasant when used in token economies in hospitals with patients who are not fully aware of what is being done to them. It is fortunate that the techniques are not as effective as their advocates would have us believe, for such methods threaten a serious loss of personal freedom.

It must not be thought, as perhaps some readers might, that psychotherapy also, if less directly, fits people into society, making them a group of contented cattle. This is not so; psychotherapy

147

and counselling should make people aware of themselves and of the difficulties which they face. This then gives them the freedom to choose for themselves. In this sense, unlike behaviour therapy, psychotherapy is value free: no advice, suggestions or recriminations are given. Indeed the only value of psychotherapy is respect for the individual. Such respect, however, in a mechanistic and objectifying society, as I have shown, becomes a political act.

The discussion has, I hope, brought the problem of the human values implicit in the scientific method as applied in psychology to human beings into the open. The experimental approach objectifies the individual concerning him as an object or mechanism which is fit for some purposes. This is the view of human beings to be found in totalitarian societies. It is contrasted with the democratic view of people who are valued simply for themselves, not what they can produce.

It is hardly surprising that experimental psychology underpins a clinical psychology and psychiatry that also sees patients as objects, this time with a flaw that requires diagnosis and treatment. Such an approach to psychiatric problems, however, is a political act in that it assumes problems within the person who ought to be happy. A psychotherapeutic approach, on the other hand, which does not regard people as objects to be happy and useful in the state, but which listens with respect to the difficulties which the patient is experiencing, may come to different conclusions, such as that the problem lies within a society that clearly requires change. Such a psychotherapeutic approach, it may be added, may well discover problems within individuals that require change. There is no antithesis of society or the individual implied in this view.

Percept-genetics, drive activation models, G analysis and values in experimental psychology

If, then, at this juncture we assume that the case has been made that experimental psychology is an approach rooted in a view of man that is mechanistic, objective and essentially inhumane there is now a case to answer. Why have I advocated, as three possible methods of enquiry, such clearly experimental psychological methods as percept-genetics, drive activation models and G analysis? If the objective approach is part of the reason why experimental psychology has failed to get to grips with what is essentially human, then surely these methods must also be worthless.

I think the critical point at issue here concerns how they are used. If, for example, a person is asked to respond to some stimuli, even if he does not have much idea what is there and then his data are collected with only the briefest of explanations that the results will help us understand the nature of personality, or some such phraseology to palm off the ignorant, then percept-genetics (which can be administered in this way) is no better than any other experimental method. It, too, is making objects of its subjects.

However, if a full explanation of what is going to occur is given to those people who are about to be administered some percept-genetic techniques, and if time is taken so that all questions are answered and a proper interpretation can be made, a totally different situation is created because both experimenter and his subjects gain from the experience. Such procedures are, of course, time consuming but nevertheless, if percept-genetics is pursued in this manner, it is difficult to argue that individuals are being treated as objects. Similar methods of discussion and interpretation can be employed with the drive activation experiments and G analysis. It should be pointed out here that this is not a primitive bartering, a sop to the conscience of the experimenter. The information that can be gained from the subjects in discussing the methods and results constitutes an important part – and one that is irreplaceable – of the data.

Psychometrics, as we have seen, can be a truly objective approach to the psychology of ability and personality. Yet even here, in a large-scale project on the measurement of personality which I carried out with Paul Barrett, we gave complete feedback to every subject individually, explaining and discussing the test results with respect to their prospective careers (Kline and Barrett 1983). Most of our sample were pleased with their scores and found the exercise valuable and useful, although in this case it was a reward for submitting to twelve hours of testing. From this I think it can be concluded that the experimental methods, which are at least an initial assay into the real complexities of human psychology, can be used humanely without reducing their subjects to objects, or regarding them as machines.

149

There is a further point, however, of a more general nature concerning the values implicit in the experimental method. Essentially the scientific objectivity of the experimental method is a view of man which *per se* precludes certain questions from even arising. Thus in its extreme form the scientific perspective is inhumane. Inhumane attitudes mean that sensitive and subtle aspects of people are not only ignored but also are not even observed. In other words the experimenter is so changed that he can never be a good psychologist.

I think, as our discussion of Skinnerian behaviourism made clear, that this has happened to Skinner and his followers. It cannot be that they are so stupid that they cannot see their crude reinforcement models are a parody of human behaviour. Rather they have been compelled by science into observing only that with which science can deal. In the field of human psychology, with its infinite subtlety, it is vital to have an open mind. In this respect orthodox psychoanalysis, if not so brutalizing, is as blinkered as behaviourism.

Educational changes

However, in addition to experimental psychological methods which can deal with topics that are not trivial, I must discuss other changes in the training and selection of psychologists without which progress will be impossible and changes in the organization and structure of higher education such that it is not weighted heavily against thought and creativity, in favour of the conventional and trivial. For without these organizational and structural changes progress will again be impossible.

Changes in universities and other institutes of higher education and research

The first change that must be brought about is that promotion must not depend upon number of publications but rather on quality. This immediately would reduce the value of choosing experimental paradigms that will yield effortless large numbers of papers, variants on a useless theme. Remember it took Beethoven to write the Diabelli variations, and Beethovens are rare. This would allow researchers and psychologists time to think, to work on what truly interested them. This is not a plea for laziness or for those who cannot produce research. It is simply that without time to think work is thoughtless, and such a term accurately describes the contents of most journals.

Changes in personnel

Of course, what is really needed, although it is not a realistic possibility, is to remove almost all those with any power and authority in academic psychology. Those, that is, who support the current psychological status quo, who admire and contribute to the nonsense which I have scrutinized, work that is an affront to a civilized mind. With such men in power there is no hope.

However, by the slow progress of time even these will slip this mortal coil and require replacement. Furthermore, if promotion were to go on quality not quantity, some worthwhile changes could be fostered. What kind of psychologists are necessary for our endeavour?

The right people

As I indicated in my chapter on the scientific method in psychology one of the factors that kept it going was the nature of the psychologists themselves. Many of these were studying the subject in order to master their own problems. The denial of emotions and feelings implicit in the scientific method is a perfect defence. In addition the precision of the scientific method, its apparent accuracy is attractive to the obsessional. Thus highly repressed and obsessional people should not be encouraged into psychology. As long as these are at the helm, the inevitably less certain studies of unconscious and emotional matters will be impossible.

The true failure of experimental psychology lies in its failure to deal with the feeling side of human beings and with the unconscious. Now it is essential that psychologists are prepared to deal with this. If feelings are denied how can they be investigated? It is clear, therefore, that psychologists must be people aware of their feelings, unafraid to face them, and able to give them their place in understanding the human mind. This does not mean that the intellect and reason should be ignored. On the contrary this is equally as absurd as the present university emphasis. What is needed is recognition of both these human faculties.

How can such people be trained?

It is obvious from the analysis in this book that what is now regarded as education in experimental psychology is the worst possible training for the kind of psychologist that is needed, if the subject is to develop. Underlying many of the criticisms of experimental psychology which I have made is really a world view. The world view of man that would permit the stupidities of this subject is myopic, narrow, mechanical, poverty stricken, inhuman and inhumane. The full richness and subtlety of the human mind is lost. It is, therefore, essential before any specific psychological studies are undertaken that psychologists be educated in the humanities – in art, literature and philosophy – so that they understand the people they intend to study, and would not be affrighted at the horror of the term 'mind', resisting the logical positivism of the scientific method and yet not falling into philosophical traps so easy in the study of feelings and thoughts.

I cannot believe that anyone versed in literature and philosophy could imagine that operant conditioning could explicate behaviour or that the Prisoner's Dilemma could be of the slightest interest, or that investigation of a Boltzmann machine is anything but engineering.

With psychology as a postgraduate discipline, the various methods and techniques of scientific psychology could be quickly learned. It is not, I hope that readers have gathered, that these techniques are wrong in themselves; it is just that they are narrow and inappropriate for most of what is important in psychology. For some topics they are fine, but for unconscious processes and the study of feelings they are not well suited.

For this, the study of psychoanalytic and psychodynamic psychology is essential. Here it is important that these writers are read on their own terms. The rallying cry of the low-grade psychologist – how often it rings out in the hallowed halls of learning: 'Where is the evidence?' 'Where is the statistical analysis?' – is irrelevant. With an open mind we must seek to discover what Jung and Freud meant. Then, if possible, we must seek ways of investigating their brilliant intuitions. Such confirmations will not be science as it is conceived now in psychological laboratories, but will be science in the real sense of knowledge.

The fundamental aspects of the human mind, which scientific psychologists have avoided, must be studied. However, there are two real difficulties here. People avoid these topics because, essentially, they are painful to them. Thus it follows that training must overcome this problem. The only way so far known of enabling people to face up to their own conflicts and emotions is to have long-term therapy. Therapy is not necessarily about curing mental illness or changing behaviour, but is concerned with being able to tolerate the pain of being oneself. Once this is faced it becomes possible to contemplate it in others. Thus part of any training would be long-term therapy, not necessarily of any particular persuasion, because ultimately no matter how they are labelled or conceptualized the same unconscious conflicts have to be faced. In my view this blend of long-term psychotherapy and rigorous scientific method for people with a literate, humane background will revitalize psychology.

The second difficulty is unquestionably more troublesome to overcome. The problem lies in the nature of feeling and experience. These are so different from logical thinking and careful conceptual analysis, the normal tools of science, that it is doubtful whether the two can truly meet. My example from the study of love by Sternberg surely made that point. A logical description of love, let alone a mathematical one, cannot remotely capture the experience. This is what love poetry is about.

I do not think that this means that such rich and subtle experiences cannot be studied at all. Indeed the three experimental methods I have described in this chapter show that even now some quite complex aspects of the human psyche can be investigated. Nevertheless, such methods are only a beginning and far more flexible approaches will have to be developed than those which are currently conceived as scientific. This is part of the excitement of attempting to develop novel approaches. It will force us, as psychologists, to do some real thinking, not simply hang on the coat-tails of the natural sciences.

Finally, I would like to stress again a further consequence of my proposed changes in the education and training of psychologists in institutions which do not count words as the measure of man. I cannot believe that literate individuals who had received psychotherapy (and were not thus defending it) would consent to study trivia because it could be done well. Educated in the humanities, and trained in orthodox scientific method, such individuals would be bound to develop new methods and techniques ideal for a real psychology.

I shall draw my book to a close. I have shown that scientific psychology has avoided what are the truly human problems of existence. It has done so because it has opted for a natural scientific method that is ill suited to the investigation of such problems and because many experimental psychologists avoid their personal conflicts by resorting to the inhumanity of objective science. I have suggested a change in the education and training of psychologists, a nice blend of humanity and science, which could revitalize the subject and allow powerful investigation of what was truly human. However, at present the panoply of science reigns. Until the voice is heard throughout the land proclaiming that the glorious colours of experimental psychology are but the emperor's new clothes, there will be no progress and psychology will remain a quasi-scientific form of hermeneutics of interest only to its practitioners.

Bibliography

Ashley, D. H., Hinton, G. E., and Sejnowski, T. J. (1985) *A Learning Algorithm for Boltzmann Machines*.

Backhus, J. (1978) 'Can programming be liberated from the von Neumann style? A functional style and its algebra of programs', *Communications of the ACM*, 21:613–41.

Baddeley, A. D. (1976) *The Psychology of Memory*, New York: Basic Books.

Brown, G. W. and Harris, T. (1978) *Social Origins of Depression*, London: Tavistock.

Buck, J. N. (1948) 'The house tree person test', *Journal of Clinical Psychology*, 4: 151–9.

Buros, O. K. (ed.) (1978) *Mental Measurement Year Books*, Gryphon Press: New Jersey.

Catania, C. (ed.) (1985) 'Canonical Papers by B. F. Skinner', *The Behavioural and Brain Sciences*

Catania, C. (1986) 'Consequences of reinforcement', paper given at Department of Psychology, University of Exeter.

Cattell, R. B. (1957) *Personality and Motivation Structure and Measurement*, New York: World Book Co.

Cattell, R. B. (1981) *Personality and Learning Theory*, Volumes I and II, Berlin: Springer.

Cattell, R. B. and Kline, P. (1977) *The Scientific Study of Personality and Motivation*, London and New York: Academic Press.

Cattell, R. B., Horn, J. L., Sweney, A. B., and Radcliffe, J. A. (1964) *Motivational Analysis Test*, Illinois: IPAT.

Chalmers, A. F. (1978) *What is this Thing called Science?*, Milton Keynes: Open University.

Cognitive Science (1985) 9: 1. This whole volume is a symposium on massively parallel processing models.

Collins, A. M. and Loftus, E. F. (1975) 'A spreading-activation theory of semantic processing', *Psychological Review*, 82: 407–28.

Cooper, C. and Kline, P. (1986) 'An Evaluation of the Defence Mechanism Test', *British Journal of Psychology*, 77: 19–31.

Danto, A. C. (1984) 'Skinner on the verbal behaviour of verbal behaviourists', *Behavioural and Brain Sciences*, 7: 555–6.

Dixon, N. F. (1971) *Subliminal Perception: The Nature of a Controversy*, New York: McGraw-Hill.

Eiser, J. R. (1980) *Cognitive Social Psychology*, New York: McGraw-Hill.

Eysenck, M. W. (1984) *A Handbook of Cognitive Psychology*, London: Erlbaum.

Farrell, B. A. (1982) *The Standing of Psychoanalysis*, Oxford: Oxford University Press.

Feldman, J. A. (1985) 'Connectionist models and their applications', *Cognitive Science*, 9: 1–2.

Fenichel, O. (1945) *Psychoanalytic Theory of Neurosis*, New York: Norton.

Festinger. L. (1957) *A Theory of Cognitive Dissonance*, Stanford: Stanford University Press.

Grünbaum, A. (1984) *The Foundations of Psychoanalysis – A Philosophical Critique*, Berkeley: University of California Press.

Heider, F. (1958) *The Psychology of Interpersonal Relations*, New York: Wiley.

Hinde, R. A. (1974) *Biological Bases of Human Social Behaviour*, New York: McGraw-Hill.

Jensen, A. R. (1981) *Bias in Mental Testing*, New York: Free Press.

Kamin, L. F. (1974) *The Science and Politics of IQ*, New York: Wiley.

Kline, P. (1972) *Fact and Fantasy in Freudian Theory*, London: Methuen.

Kline, P. (1975) *Psychology of Vocational Guidance*, London: Batsford.

Kline, P. and Barrett, P. (1983) 'The factors in personality questionnaires among normal subjects', *Advances in Behavioural Research and Therapy*, 5:141–202.

Kline, P. and Cooper, C. (1977) 'A percept-genetic study of some defence mechanisms in the test PN', *Scandinavian Journal of Psychology*, 18:148–52.

Kragh, U. (1969) *The Defence Mechanism Test*, Testforlaget: Stockholm.

Kragh, U. and Smith, G. S. (1970) *Percept-Genetic Analysis*, Lund: Gleerups.

Kuhn, I. S. (1975) 'Logic of discovery or psychology of research', in I. Lakatos and A. Musgrave (eds), *Criticism and the Growth of Knowledge*, Cambridge: Cambridge University Press.

Lakatos, I. and Musgrave, A. (eds) (1975) *Criticism and the Growth of Knowledge*, Cambridge: Cambridge University Press.

McClelland, J. L. (1985) 'Putting knowledge in its place: a scheme for programming parallel processing structures on the fly', *Cognitive Science*, 9,1:113–46.

Marr, D. (1982) *Vision*, New York: Freeman.

Meehl, P. E. (1984) 'Radical behaviourism and mental events: four methodological queries', *Behavioural and Brain Sciences*, 7: 563–4.

Milgram, S. (1974) *Obedience to Authority*, London: Tavistock.

Morton, J. (1987) *Bulletin of the British Psychological Society*, A19.

Pagel, M. D. and Davidson, A. R. (1984) 'A comparison of three social psychological models of attitude and behavioural plan: prediction of contraceptive behaviour', *Journal of Personality and Social Psychology*, 47:517–33.

Pickering, P. (1986) *The Psychosocial Characteristics of Long-Term Tranquilliser Users*, PhD Thesis, University of Exeter.

The Plowden Report (1986) London: HMSO.

Popper, K. (1968) *The Logic of Scientific Discovery*, London: Hutchinson.

Rachman, S. (1977) 'The conditioning theory of fear acquisition: a critical examination', *Behaviour Research and Therapy*, 15:375–87.

Sabbah, D. (1985) 'Computing with connections in visual recognition of origami objects', *Cognitive Science*, 9,1:25–50.

Sharpe, T. (1981) *The Wilt Alternative*, London: Pan Books.

Silverman, L.H. (1983) 'The drive activation method', in J. Masling (ed.) *Empirical Studies of Psychoanalytic Theories*, Hillsdale: Analytic Press.

Sjoback, H. (1967) *The Defence Mechanism Test*, Lund: The Calytographic Foundation.

Smail, D. (1984) *Illusion and Reality*, London: J. M. Dent.

Spence, D. P., Klein, L., and Fernandez, R. J. (1986) 'Size and shape of the subliminal window', in V. Hentschel, G.J.W. Smith, and J. G. Draguns (eds) (1986) *The Roots of Perception*, Amsterdam.

Sternberg, R. J. and Grojek, S. (1984) *The Nature of Love*

Thurstone, L.L. (1928) 'Attitudes can be measured', *American Journal of Sociology*, 33:529–54.

Tulving, E. (1983) *Elements of Episodic Memory*, Oxford: Oxford University Press.

Vernon, P. E. (1951) *The Measurement of Abilities*, London: University of London Press.

Waltz, D. L. and Pollack, J. B. (1985) 'Massively parallel parsing: a strongly interactive model of natural language interpretation', *Cognitive Science*, 9,1:51–74.

Westerlundh, B. (1976) *Aggression, Anxiety and Defence*, Lund: Gleerups.

Wilson, O. (1975) *Sociobiology*, Boston: Harvard University Press.

Wilson, O. (1978) *On Human Nature*, Boston: Harvard University Press.

Index